Industrial Automation in the Era of AI:

How Industry Reinvents Itself

Dr. Len Mei

Contents

Preface

The manufacturing industry stands at the precipice of a transformative era, driven by the relentless advancement of automation technologies. The book "Industrial Automation in the Era of AI" delves into the profound impact of automation on modern manufacturing, exploring its role in reshaping production processes, enhancing efficiency, and enabling unprecedented levels of precision and scalability. Automation is no longer a luxury but a necessity for manufacturers striving to remain competitive in an increasingly complex and dynamic global market.

This book is designed to provide a comprehensive understanding of the architecture of automation, which is built on three foundational pillars: "equipment automation", "factory operation automation", and "data automation". Each pillar plays a critical role in creating a seamless, interconnected manufacturing ecosystem.

Equipment automation focuses on the optimization of individual machines, ensuring they operate at peak efficiency with minimal human intervention. Factory operation automation extends this concept to entire production lines, integrating robotics, material handling systems, and advanced control systems to streamline workflows. Data automation, the third pillar, leverages the power of artificial intelligence (AI), machine learning, and digital twin technologies to analyze vast amounts of data, enabling predictive maintenance, real-time quality control, and data-driven decision-making.

One of the most exciting developments in automation is the integration of AI and digital twin technologies. AI algorithms analyze data from sensors, machines, and production systems to identify patterns, predict failures, and optimize processes. Digital twins, virtual replicas of physical assets, allow manufacturers to simulate and test production scenarios in a risk-free environment, enabling them to fine-tune operations before implementing changes on the factory floor. Together, AI and digital twins are revolutionizing data automation, providing manufacturers with unparalleled insights into their operations.

Automation is not confined to the factory floor; it extends its influence across the entire value chain. From supply chain management to product design, customer service, and market analysis, automation creates a seamless link between these critical functions and the factory.

Design automation ensures that the product designed is manufacturable. Additive manufacturing makes possible that prototype is ready soon after design is finished. Automated supply chains ensure timely delivery of raw materials, while AI-driven design tools enable the creation of innovative, high-quality products.

Customer service is enhanced through automated systems that provide real-time support and feedback, while market analysis tools help manufacturers anticipate demand and adjust production accordingly.

Quality control, operations, and maintenance are three areas where automation has made significant strides. Automated quality control systems use sensors and AI to detect defects in real time, ensuring that only products meeting the highest standards reach the market.

In operations, automation optimizes production schedules, reduces downtime, and improves resource utilization. Predictive maintenance, powered by data automation, minimizes equipment failures and extends the lifespan of machinery, reducing costs and improving reliability.

The benefits of automation are manifold. It increases productivity, reduces labor costs, enhances product quality, and improves workplace safety. Automation also enables manufacturers to respond quickly to changing market demands, providing a competitive edge in today's fast-paced business environment. Furthermore, automation plays a pivotal role in the realization of Industry 4.0, the fourth industrial revolution characterized by smart factories, interconnected systems, and data-driven decision-making.

In this context, the concept of the "Lights-out Factory" – a fully automated facility that operates without human intervention – is no longer a distant dream but a tangible reality for many forward-thinking manufacturers.

The scope of automation in Industry 4.0 is vast, encompassing everything from advanced robotics and IoT enabled devices to cloud computing and big data analytics.

As manufacturers embrace these technologies, they are unlocking new levels of efficiency, flexibility, and innovation. However, the journey toward full automation is not without challenges. It requires significant investment, a skilled workforce, and a commitment to continuous improvement.

This book aims to guide manufacturers through this journey, providing insights, strategies, and best practices for successfully implementing automation in their operations.

"Industrial Automation in the Era of AI" is a testament to the transformative power of automation in shaping the future of manufacturing. It is a call to action for manufacturers to embrace automation, not as a mere tool, but as a strategic imperative for growth and sustainability.

This book is for both average readers who are interested in the state of art industrial development and the seasoned industry professional. Welcome to the future of manufacturing. Welcome to the age of automation.

Chapter I. Industry 4.0, Automation and AI

The convergence of "Industry 4.0", "automation" and "AI" is revolutionizing the manufacturing and business landscape, ushering in an era of smart factories, interconnected systems, and data-driven decision-making. Industry 4.0, often referred to as the fourth industrial revolution, represents a paradigm shift in how manufacturing and business processes are designed, implemented, and optimized.

At its core, Industry 4.0 leverages advanced technologies such as the "Internet of Things **Error! Bookmark not defined.**(IoT)"**Error! Bookmark not defined.**, "artificial intelligence (AI)", "big data analytics", "robotics", and "cloud and edge computing**Error! Bookmark not defined.**" to create intelligent, self-optimizing production and administrative systems.

Automation, a cornerstone of Industry 4.0, plays a pivotal role in enabling these advancements, driving efficiency, precision, and scalability across the manufacturing value chain.

Section 1.01   What is Industry 4.0?

The concept of "Industry 4.0" was first introduced as part of a high-tech strategy initiative by the German government in 2011. The term "Industry 4.0" was officially coined at the Hannover Fair, one of the world's largest industrial trade fairs, to describe the fourth industrial revolution driven by the integration of digital technologies into manufacturing and industrial processes.

The notion of Industry 4.0 was popularized by a working group formed by the German government, academia, and industry leaders. The goal was to enhance Germany's competitiveness in manufacturing by leveraging advanced technologies.

While Industry 4.0 originated in Germany, its principles and technologies have been adopted worldwide, and become a worldwide standard and the common goal for the next industrial revolution.

Industry 4.0 represents the ongoing transformation of traditional manufacturing and industrial practices through the integration of advanced digital technologies. It builds on the foundations of the first three industrial revolutions—mechanization (1st), mass production (2nd), and automation (3rd)—by introducing smart, interconnected systems that leverage data, artificial intelligence (AI), and the Internet of Things

Industry 4.0 is the integration of digital technologies into manufacturing and business processes, creating a connected ecosystem where machines, systems, and humans communicate and collaborate in real time.

Unlike previous industrial revolutions, which focused on mechanization, mass production, and computerization, Industry 4.0 emphasizes "smart manufacturing" – the use of data and automation to optimize production processes and create value.

In Industry 4.0, all production elements such as machines, devices, systems, different parties in the production environment are interconnected through IoT**Error! Bookmark not defined.**, enabling seamless communication and data exchange.

In addition, they are also connected to the elements outside of the factory, including business, supply chain, customer service and many others. This is because production is not an isolated event. Production automation is not complete without automating its related business process, for example, supply chain management system, production planning and scheduling, etc.

The connectivity provides the exchanges of data and information, including decisions. Most of the decisions are driven by data using advanced analytics and AI algorithms. These tools process vast amounts of data, providing actionable insights for optimizing operations.

Industry 4.0 factories are smart because they make decisions autonomously based on huge amount of data and rigorous algorithms, reducing reliance on centralized control. In addition, on the factory floor, advanced AI enabled robotics allows humans and machines working together more effectively.

Virtual replicas of physical assets creates digital twin which allows manufacturers to simulate and optimize processes in a risk-free environment. Before any decision is made, digital twin allows us to see the result and consequence of such a decision. It further optimizes the decision to obtain the best result.

Section 1.02   The Role of Automation in Industry 4.0

Industry 4.0 operates smart factories: Highly digitized and connected production facilities where machines and systems communicate and make decisions autonomously.

Industry 4.0 is characterized by several key principles:

- Interconnectivity: Machines, devices, sensors, and people are connected through the Internet of Things **Error! Bookmark not defined.** (IoT**Error! Bookmark not defined.**), enabling seamless communication and data exchange.   Information

- Transparency: Data collected from sensors and devices is analyzed and visualized in real-time, providing operators with actionable insights.
- Technical Assistance: Systems assist humans in decision-making, problem-solving, and performing complex or unsafe tasks.
- Decentralized Decision-Making: Cyber-physical systems **Error! Bookmark not defined.**(CPS **Error! Bookmark not defined.**) can make decisions and perform tasks autonomously, reducing the need for human intervention.
- Automated Business Processes: Automated business processes leverage technology to streamline, optimize, and execute tasks with minimal human intervention, enhancing efficiency, accuracy, and scalability.
- Interoperability: Seamless communication and collaboration between different systems, devices, and stakeholders.

In order to achieve the above stated objectives, many cutting-edge technologies form the backbone of Industry 4.0:

- Internet of Things connects physical devices and machines to the internet, enabling them to collect, share, and analyze data. IoT allows machines to communicate with each other and with central systems.
- Artificial Intelligence (AI) and Machine Learning (ML): AI and ML based algorithms analyze vast amounts of data to optimize processes, predict outcomes, and enable autonomous decision-making.
- Big Data **Error! Bookmark not defined.**and Analytics: The massive amounts of data generated and collected by IoT **Error! Bookmark not defined.** devices are analyzed to uncover patterns, trends, and insights that drive efficiency and innovation.
- Cyber-Physical Systems (CPS **Error! Bookmark not defined.**): CPS's integrate physical processes with

digital systems, enabling real-time monitoring and control. Examples include smart grids and autonomous vehicles.

- Cloud and Edge Computing: Cloud and edge platforms provide the infrastructure for storing, processing, and analyzing data, enabling scalability and collaboration.
- Additive Manufacturing (3D Printing): 3D printing allows for the rapid prototyping and production of complex parts, reducing waste and enabling customization.
- Augmented Reality (AR) and Virtual Reality (VR): AR and VR technologies are used for training, maintenance, and design, providing immersive experiences that enhance productivity and accuracy.
- Robotics and Automation: Advanced robots and automated systems perform tasks with precision and efficiency, reducing the need for human labor in hazardous or repetitive tasks.

These new technologies provide a new level of automation in the manufacturing not seen before. As AI continues to evolve, Industry 4.0 also evolves with it. It can be said that Industry 4.0 is the ultimate goal of industrial automation.

With unprecedented automation, Industry 4.0 offers huge improvement from the current state of manufacturing, such as:

- Increased Efficiency: Automation and data-driven insights optimize production processes, reducing waste and downtime.
- Enhanced Flexibility: Smart factories **Error! Bookmark not defined.**can quickly adapt to changing demands, enabling mass customization and faster time-to-market.

- Improved Quality: Real-time monitoring and predictive maintenance ensure consistent product quality and reduce defects.
- Cost Savings: Automation and optimized processes lower operational costs, while predictive maintenance reduces repair expenses.
- Sustainability: Industry 4.0 technologies enable more efficient use of resources, reducing energy consumption and environmental impact.
- Product traceability: In case a product develops a defect after sales, it can be traced back to its lot number, manufacturing date, history of process steps, and the problematic step that caused the defect.

By applying these technologies to the manufacturing plant, Industry 4.0 hopes to dramatically upgrade the manufacturing capability.

As of 2025, Industry 4.0 is well underway. Many industries are adopting its core technologies such as the Internet of Things, artificial intelligence (AI), robotics, cloud computing, and big data analytics. Smart factories, predictive maintenance, and digital twins are becoming increasingly common, enabling real-time decision-making and operational efficiency. It is estimated that 50% of manufacturers have adopt IoT technologies.

By 2030, Industry 4.0 is expected to reach a mature phase, with most industries fully integrating technologies like AI, IoT, robotics, and big data analytics into their operations. Smart factories, predictive maintenance, and autonomous systems will become the norm rather than the exception.

By 2032, the global Industry 4.0 market is expected to grow significantly, reaching more than $300 billion. By then, Industry 4.0 will be in an advanced stage of adoption, with further growth anticipated in the coming years.

The integration of 5G, cloud and edge computing further accelerates the adoption of Industry 4.0. These technologies enables faster data processing, lower latency, and more robust connectivity, which are critical for smart factories and autonomous systems .

Once the Industry 4.0 becomes the main stream manufacturing standard, legacy factories which still rely on outdated infrastructure will become non-competitive and obsolete.

However, its full realization will depend on overcoming challenges related to technology, workforce, and infrastructure. The transition to Industry 4.0 requires a workforce skilled in digital technologies. The global workforce in the Industry 4.0 sector is expected to exceed 1 million employees, with significant investments in training programs to address the skills gap.

By addressing these barriers, industries can fully harness the potential of Industry 4.0 to drive efficiency, innovation, and sustainability. For more detailed insights, you can refer to the sources cited in this response.

Industry 4.0 represents a paradigm shift in how industries operate, driven by the integration of advanced digital technologies. By enabling smarter, more connected, and more efficient systems, Industry 4.0 has the potential to revolutionize manufacturing, energy, healthcare, and beyond. However, realizing its full potential requires addressing challenges such as cybersecurity, workforce transformation, and data privacy.

As industries continue to embrace Industry 4.0, they will unlock new opportunities for innovation, efficiency, and sustainability, shaping the future of the global economy.

However, the evolution of industry will not end with Industry 4.0. In the 2030's, Industry 4.0 will evolve into

Industry 5.0, which emphasizes human-centric, ethical, and sustainable practices. This shift will likely be more pronounced by 2035, as industries focus on resilience, inclusivity, and environmental responsibility.

While Industry 4.0 focused on automation, data exchange, and smart factories, Industry 5.0 reintroduces the human element into the equation. It emphasizes collaboration between humans and machines, rather than replacing human labor with automation. Additionally, Industry 5.0 places greater importance on societal and environmental goals, moving beyond mere economic efficiency .

Section 1.03 Intelligent Manufacturing

Intelligent Manufacturing or sometimes known as smart factory is one of the most important features of Industry 4.0. It refers to the use of smart technologies to create manufacturing systems that are capable of self-learning, self-optimization, and autonomous decision-making. It combines advanced technologies such as artificial intelligence (AI), the Internet of Things (IoT), big data, robotics, and cloud computing to create highly efficient, adaptive, and self-optimizing manufacturing systems. It is a core component of Industry 4.0, and focuses on leveraging data-driven insights and automation to transform traditional manufacturing processes.

Unlike traditional manufacturing, which relies on fixed processes and human intervention, intelligent manufacturing systems are dynamic, interconnected, and data-driven. Most of the time, minimum human intervention is required. They enable real-time monitoring, analysis, and control of production processes, leading to improved efficiency, quality, and flexibility.

To build intelligent manufacturing, one would need some basic components in the factory to carry out three steps: data collection, data analysis, decision execution. To do so, the factory needs to be equipped with:

- Connectivity: All equipment, workstation, materials transport system, warehouse, manufacturing execution system, need to be interconnected through Internet of Things (IoT) to collect and exchange data in real-time. This connectivity enables seamless communication between different components of the manufacturing process.
- Big Data Analytics: Intelligent manufacturing relies on the analysis of large datasets to gain insights into production processes, supply chains, and customer demand. In the most advanced manufacturing site, AI and ML algorithms are used to analyze data to identify patterns, predict outcomes, and generate decisions for the optimized processes.
- Control mechanism: Such decision is to be implemented into the production line through a feedback loop to allow these decisions to be executed and carried out automatically. This feedback loop allows the factory to run by itself.

These capabilities are accomplished by many systems in a smart factory. Each system carries out one or more of the three functions mentioned above. For example, Cyber-Physical System (CPS) integrates physical machinery with digital systems, enabling real-time monitoring and control.

Advanced robotics and automation systems perform complex tasks with precision and adaptability. Collaborative robots (cobots) work alongside humans to enhance productivity.

Cloud and Edge platforms provide scalable storage and computing power for data processing, analytics, and collaboration across global operations. Edge computing will also play an increasingly important role in processing data at the edge (closer to the source) for better latency and enable real-time decision-making.

AI, residing in the Cloud and Edge platforms, will play an increasingly central role in automating and optimizing manufacturing processes. Virtual replicas of physical systems, known as Digital Twin, will enable real-time monitoring, simulation, and optimization.

While challenges such as high costs and cyber security risks exist, the benefits of intelligent manufacturing far outweigh the obstacles. As technology continues to evolve, intelligent manufacturing will play a central role in driving innovation, sustainability, and competitiveness in the global manufacturing landscape.

Section 1.04   Manufacturing Automation and Business Automation

Industry 4.0 embraces both the automation in the production floor and related business processes. These two aspects of automation complement each other. While manufacturing automation and business automation are closely related practices, their scopes are different.

Manufacturing automation focuses on automating machines and systems to perform production tasks, while the business process automation focuses on the tasks of business workflows and procedures.

Manufacturing automation uses control systems, machinery, and software to automate production processes. The most basic and well-known systems include:

- Robotics: Used for repetitive tasks like welding or painting.

- CNC Machines: Computer-controlled machines for precision cutting and machining.
- Conveyor Systems: Automated systems for moving materials and products through the production line.

These systems replace human labors, improve efficiency and safety, and increase consistency in manufacturing operations. The primary goal is to increase productivity, reduce costs, and minimize errors.

These kinds of automation are task-specific. Machines and robots are programmed to perform specific tasks, such as assembly, welding, or packaging. Smart factories can quickly adapt to changes in demand, product design, or production requirements. As we will discuss later that in today's smart factory, the manufacturing automation is much more than just robotics, CNC machines and conveyors.

On the other hand, business automation refers to the use of technology to perform repetitive tasks, streamline and automate operations and workflow, and improve efficiency within an organization.

By leveraging software, artificial intelligence, and machine learning, businesses can automate processes such as data entry, customer service, inventory management, and financial reporting. This reduces human error, saves time, and allows employees to focus on higher-value tasks that require creativity and critical thinking.

Business automation also enhances customer experiences through tools like chatbots, personalized marketing, and automated support systems. For example, e-commerce platforms use automation to recommend products based on user behavior, while logistics companies optimize delivery routes using AI-driven algorithms.

Additionally, business automation provides valuable data insights, enabling businesses to make informed decisions and adapt to market trends quickly.

Overall, business automation is as powerful and important as the manufacturing automation for driving growth, improving productivity, and staying competitive in a fast-paced, technology-driven world. When implemented strategically, it can transform operations and create long-term value for organizations.

The combination of manufacturing and business automation provides a streamlined operation throughout the industry.

Section 1.05   Three Types of Manufacturing Automation

Automation in manufacturing falls into three major categories: Equipment Automation, Factory Operation Automation and Data Automation.

Equipment automation focuses on the automation of individual machines or tools used in the manufacturing process. It involves the use of sensors, controllers, and software to monitor and control equipment operations. The data collected during the process are sent to the specialized server for analysis. It provides real-time feedback of the equipment and process status. Any deviation raises alarm immediately.

At the same time, the connectivity of equipment with server also provides the automatic operation and control of the production. When a production lot is loaded into the equipment, the lot ID is immediately verified. The process receipt is then downloaded to the equipment to start the process. For different products requiring different process recipes, this provides flexibility.

In addition, equipment automation allows predictive and preventive maintenance. We will discuss more in the later part of this book. The primary goal is to enhance the performance, reliability, and efficiency of machinery.

Factory automation encompasses the automation of entire production lines or facilities. It involves the integration of various systems and platforms, both hardware and software, such as robotics, conveyor systems, material handling equipment, line balance algorithm to create a seamless and efficient manufacturing environment.

The semi-finished products being processed in the production line are called WIP (Work-in-Progress). Depending on the complexity of the production process, the total time required to complete the production, known as cycle time, can be from few days to several months.

A large amount of WIP is accumulated in the factory. These accumulated WIP represents idling capital from financial point of view. Faster production cycletime can release some amount of these capitals for more productive use. In general, the capital amount of WIP is the total cost of the product produced in one month multiplied by half cycle time in month. For example, if the cost of products produced in a factory per month is $100 m and the cycletime is two months, the WIP value is $100 m.

Factory automation aims to optimize the flow of materials, reduce cycletime, and improve overall productivity, without adding additional resources to the factory.

Data automation refers to the use of software and algorithms to collect, process, and analyze data generated during the manufacturing process. It enables manufacturers to make data-driven decisions, identify inefficiencies, and improve product quality. Data automation is essential for implementing predictive maintenance, quality control, and supply chain optimization.

The data collected in the factory includes product data, production data, quality data, equipment data, technology data and many others. All these data are generated on the factory floor and collected by IoT and sent to the centralized servers.

These data are fed into different algorithms for analysis and generate immediate feedback for decisions. The generated decision can either by used to control systems on the factory floor or in the report form for management review. When AI is deployed, these data are fed into the digital twin for real time simulation and optimization to control the operation.

Section 1.06   Benefits of Industry 4.0

The integration manufacturing and business automation in the Industry 4.0 offers numerous benefits for manufacturers:

- Increased Productivity: Automated systems operate faster and more efficiently than manual systems, leading to higher output and reduced production times.
- Improved Quality: Automation ensures consistent and precise execution of tasks, reducing the risk of defects and improving product quality.
- Reduced Costs: Automation reduces labor costs, minimizes waste, and optimizes resource utilization, leading to significant cost savings.
- Enhanced Flexibility: Automated systems can be easily reprogrammed to accommodate changes in product design or production requirements, enabling mass customization. Flexibility allows smart factory to product customized product.

- Predictive Maintenance: IoT and AI enable predictive maintenance, reducing downtime and extending the lifespan of equipment.
- Real-Time Decision-Making: Data analytics and AI provide real-time insights, enabling manufacturers to make informed decisions and respond quickly to changing conditions.
- Sustainability: Automation optimizes energy consumption and reduces waste, contributing to more sustainable manufacturing practices.

Section 1.07 The Future of Industry 4.0 and Automation

The future of Industry 4.0 and automation is bright, with emerging technologies such as "5G", "edge computing", and "quantum computing" poised to further enhance the capabilities of smart factories.

These technologies will enable faster data processing, greater connectivity, and more advanced AI algorithms, paving the way for fully autonomous factories and lights-out manufacturing.

IoT connects machines, devices, and systems through sensors and communication networks, enabling real-time data collection and exchange. In a smart factory, IoT devices monitor equipment performance, track inventory, and optimize production processes.

Advanced robotics automate repetitive and labor-intensive tasks, while cobots work alongside humans to enhance productivity and safety.

Big data analytics processes vast amounts of data generated by IoT devices and other sources, providing insights into production efficiency, quality control, and supply chain management.

AI algorithms analyze data from IoT devices and other sources to identify patterns, predict outcomes, and optimize operations. Machine learning enables systems to improve their performance over time without explicit programming.

Cloud computing enables the storage and processing of data in remote servers, providing manufacturers with scalable and cost-effective solutions for managing their operations.

Digital twins are virtual replicas of physical assets, processes, or systems. They allow manufacturers to simulate and optimize production scenarios in a risk-free environment.

Lights-out factories, which operate without human intervention, represent the ultimate realization of Industry 4.0 and automation. These factories rely entirely on automated systems, robotics, and AI to perform all production tasks. While still in the early stages of adoption, lights-out factories offer the potential for 24/7 production, reduced labor costs, and unparalleled efficiency.

The journey toward Industry 4.0 and automation is not just about adopting new technologies; it is about reimagining the future of manufacturing. By embracing this transformation, manufacturers can position themselves at the forefront of the fourth industrial revolution, shaping the future of the industry and driving progress for generations to come.

Chapter II. Equipment Automation

The primary purpose of equipment automation is to enhance the performance and reliability of individual machines. By automating equipment, manufacturers can reduce manual intervention, minimize human error, and ensure consistent output. Automated equipment is capable of performing repetitive tasks with high precision, which is particularly beneficial in industries such as automotive, electronics, and pharmaceuticals.

Equipment automation starts with building smart equipment. Smart equipment has the capability of collecting data, processing data and transmitting data. In a smart factory, all equipment is interconnected.

The performance of equipment can be fully represented in its data. In the mechanical equipment, the mechanical torque, displacement, velocity, acceleration, momentum, moment of inertia, etc. reflect the performance of equipment. In a chemical plant, the equipment has important characteristics such as temperature, pressure, gas flow, pumping speed, etc. By collecting and monitoring these data in real-time, one can tell the performance of equipment in real time. Using Statistical Process Control method, any deviation detected implies that either process or equipment has developed a potential problem, and requires an action. The action may mean to adjust equipment operating parameters through automatic control or shut down the equipment for maintenance.

In order to collect data, sensors are embedded in the equipment monitor parameters such as temperature, pressure, vibration, and speed. This data is transmitted to a central system for analysis, enabling manufacturers to identify potential issues before they escalate into major problems. For example, if a machine's temperature exceeds a predefined threshold, the system can trigger an alert or shut down the equipment to prevent damage.

Automated equipment is equipped with controllers that regulate its operation based on predefined parameters. These controllers can adjust settings such as speed, force, and position to ensure optimal performance. For instance, in a CNC (Computer Numerical Control) machine, the controller directs the movement of the cutting tool to produce parts with high precision. By automating equipment operation, manufacturers can achieve greater consistency and reduce the risk of defects.

Equipment automation plays a crucial role in increasing machine uptime. Automated systems can detect and address issues such as wear and tear, misalignment, or component failure before they lead to unplanned downtime.

Section 2.01   Predictive and Preventive Maintenance

Equipment maintenance is one of the largest cost of the ownership (COO) of the equipment besides depreciation. Its cost incurs in several aspects:

First, when the equipment is shut down, it is removed from production. It represents the loss of productivity. Second, it requires resources to bring it up. These resources include engineering time and spare parts.

In addition, if the equipment is shut down because equipment malfunction occurs, some WIP's are already being damaged due to the time lag from the occurrence of malfunction to its detection.

The damaged WIP needs to be handled, either by reworking or scrapping. It takes additional resources to do so. Reworking requires additional resources and scrapping the

WIP further invalidates all the work which has been performed on the WIP.

To prevent this problem, one need to detect the equipment malfunction in real-time before the damage occurs. This can be achieved by the so-called the Predictive Maintenance. It is contrast to unscheduled maintenance which reactive to the damaged WIP.

The traditional Preventive Maintenance (PM) involves scheduled, routine maintenance activities aimed at preventing equipment failure before it occurs. It is based on time, usage, or operational cycles.

Preventive maintenance (PM) is performed at regular intervals, such as weekly, monthly, or after a certain number of operating hours, regardless of the actual condition of the equipment. Examples include changing oil in a car every 5,000 miles, replacing air filters in HVAC systems every 6 months, and inspecting and lubricating machinery every 1,000 hours of operation.

Even with the rigorous Preventive Maintenance, it is hard to prevent equipment going down unexpectedly. When it happens, it required Unscheduled Maintenance.

The Predictive Maintenance, on the other hand, performs maintenance as soon as it detects the abnormal equipment performance from the data collected in real-time before the damage occurs.

In doing so, it can prevent equipment from doing the damage to the production and providing maintenance when needed.

In order to do so, one has to collect the data from the equipment and perform analysis in real time. The analysis has to predict accurately when and what kind of performance deviation is imminent, based on the actual condition of the equipment. The accuracy of the prediction depends on the accuracy of the data and the prediction model. If the accuracy is not there, its prediction is not effective, which can lead to unnecessary shut down or miss the malfunction altogether.

Predictive maintenance relies on sensors, IoT devices, and advanced analytics to monitor equipment health. Maintenance is performed as needed, rather than on a fixed schedule. Examples include monitoring vibration levels in rotating machinery to detect imbalance or misalignment, using thermal imaging to identify overheating components, and analyzing oil samples to detect contamination or wear.

The advantages of predictive maintenance include reducing unnecessary scheduled maintenance by focusing on actual equipment condition, minimizing downtime by addressing issues before they cause failure, and optimizing maintenance costs by avoiding premature part replacements. Since the data already predicts the potential faulty area, the time spent on diagnosis is also drastically reduced.

In order to perform the Predictive Maintenance effectively, it is important to have the correct fault detection model. Such a fault detection model contains a large database of the equipment and can correlate the equipment data to the potential faults by using statistical control method in real time. The use of AI and ML further improves the accuracy of model prediction. It can even offer precise diagnosis as to the procedures to be performed and spare parts to be replaced to fix the problem.

Equipment automation also brings other benefits to the equipment. Manufacturers can significantly increase equipment throughput. By analyzing the speed of equipment at every single step, the bottleneck step can be improved. Automated machines can operate at higher speeds and with greater accuracy than manual systems, enabling faster production cycles. Additionally, automated equipment can operate continuously without the need for breaks, further boosting productivity. For example, in a bottling plant, automated filling machines can fill thousands of bottles per hour, far exceeding the capacity of manual operations.

Section 2.02   Fault Detection Model

The accuracy of prediction depends on the data collected and the soundness of fault detection model used. The most commonly used technique is to use the Statistical Process Control (SPC) model. It involves using statistical methods to monitor and control a process, ensuring it operates within specified limits. SPC helps detect faults or anomalies by analyzing process data and identifying variations that may indicate problems.

The first step in building such model is to identify the key process parameters or variables to monitor (e.g., temperature, pressure, dimensions, or defect rates).

The historical data from the process is used to establish a baseline. Ensure the data is accurate, consistent, and representative of normal operating conditions.

Of course, one must to make sure that the sensors, IoT devices, or manual measurements used to collect real-time data during the process are truly accurate.

Control charts are used to determine if the process is stable (in control) or unstable (out of control). Common control charts include X-bar and R charts for monitoring the mean and range of a process, Individual and Moving Range (I-MR) charts for individual measurements, P-charts and C-charts for monitoring defect rates or counts. The model also calculates the Upper Control Limit (UCL) and Lower Control Limit (LCL) based on historical data.

During the monitoring, look for patterns or signals that indicate faults, such as Out-of-control points: Data points outside the control limits, consistent upward or downward movement of data points, repeating patterns in the data. There are popular rules used in the industry, such as: Six Sigma, 7-Point Rule in Statistical Control, in which if seven consecutive data points in a control chart fall on one side of the mean (either above or below), it indicates a potential shift in the process that requires investigation, both were invented by Motorola.

When a fault is detected (e.g., a point outside control limits), such a deviation must be correlated to a given fault or faults. The model will have to provide the database of faults using various techniques such as Fishbone diagrams, Pareto analysis, etc.

Once the root cause is identified, the equipment automation will have to make a decision either to alter the process, take self-corrective actions or to inform the engineer to shut down the equipment to bring the process back into control.

Such fault detection model should be dynamic. It requires regularly review the SPC model and update it based on new data or process changes.

Section 2.03   Overall Equipment Efficiency

Overall Equipment Efficiency (OEE) is a critical metric in manufacturing and production environments, used to evaluate the effectiveness and productivity of equipment and processes. It provides a holistic view of how well a manufacturing operation is performing by measuring the percentage of planned production time that is truly productive.

The term OEE is also used as a methodology and a powerful tool for identifying inefficiencies, reducing waste, and improving overall performance. It is widely adopted across industries as a benchmark for continuous improvement and operational excellence.

The metric OEE is calculated by multiplying three key factors: Availability, Performance, and Quality. Each of these components represents a different aspect of production efficiency, and together they provide a comprehensive picture of equipment performance.

1. Availability: Availability measures the actual operating time of equipment compared to the planned production time. It accounts for downtime caused by equipment failures, setup adjustments, and other unplanned stoppages. High availability indicates that equipment is running as much as possible, minimizing downtime.

Availability =

(Operating Time/Planned Production Time) × 100

2. Performance: Performance evaluates how efficiently the equipment is running during its operating time. It considers factors such as speed losses, minor stoppages, and reduced cycle times. A high performance score means the equipment is operating close to its maximum potential speed.

Performance =

(Actual Production / Ideal Production) × 100

3. Quality: Quality measures the proportion of good units produced compared to the total units started. It accounts for defects, rework, and scrap. A high quality score indicates that the process is producing a high yield of defect-free products.

Quality =

(Good Units / Total Units Produced) × 100

The metric OEE is

OEE =

Availability Performance Quality

OEE, as a tool, provides several benefits to manufacturing operations:

- Identifies Losses: By breaking down efficiency into Availability, Performance, and Quality, OEE helps pinpoint specific areas of loss, such as downtime, slow cycles, or defects.
- Drives Continuous Improvement: OEE serves as a baseline for improvement initiatives, enabling teams to set targets and track progress over time.
- Enhances Decision-Making: Data-driven insights from OEE analysis support better decision-making regarding equipment maintenance, process optimization, and resource allocation.
- Increases Productivity: By addressing inefficiencies, OEE helps maximize equipment utilization and output, leading to higher productivity and profitability.

Overall Equipment Efficiency (OEE) is a vital metric for assessing and improving manufacturing performance. By analyzing Availability, Performance, and Quality, OEE provides actionable insights to reduce waste, optimize processes, and enhance productivity. When effectively implemented, OEE becomes a cornerstone of operational excellence, driving sustainable growth and competitiveness in the manufacturing sector.

Performing the Overall Equipment Efficiency (OEE) methodology involves a structured approach to measure and improve the effectiveness of manufacturing equipment. Equipment automation can greatly boost OEE.

First, equipment automation allows to collect detailed equipment data such as total time the equipment is scheduled to operate, actual time the equipment is running, the theoretical fastest time to produce one unit, number of units manufactured during the operating time, number of units that do not meet quality standards. These data allow us to calculate the metric OEE.

Furthermore, one can get detailed information about downtime due to breakdowns, setup, or maintenance, slow cycles, minor stoppages, or idling, defects, rework, or scrap. Such detailed data allow one to address the root causes of losses, for example, to reduce downtime through preventive maintenance, to optimize machine speed and reduce minor stoppages, to improve processes to minimize defects.

Benchmarking OEE of two identical equipment also allow one to find the difference and bring the less performed unit to the standard of better performed unit. Scale the OEE methodology to other equipment or production lines can achieve broader impact.

Factory can effectively use the OEE methodology to enhance productivity, reduce waste, and achieve operational excellence.

Chapter III. Factory Automation I - Components

Factory automation, short for factory operation automation, focuses on optimizing the movement of work-in-progress (WIP) materials through the production process. The purpose of automation is to reduce the time and manpower required to operate the machinery and factory to improve productivity and efficiency. As an added benefit, factory automation also greatly improves factory safety because dangerous jobs are all performed by automation.

Factory operation needs to optimize all aspects of its performance. The outcome of a factory is measured much more than just its output per day. And automation is more than automatic WIP transport system.

Factory automation is composed of hardware and software systems. The hardware and software combination forms the basic building blocks of the factory automation. These building blocks are so called the components of automation. Different components build functional blocks of the automation platforms and systems, which serve for specific automation purposes.

In this chapter, we will discuss the most important components of the factory automation. In the next chapter, we will discuss the platforms and systems what perform factory automation.

Section 3.01 Performance of a Factory

Benchmarking the success of a factory involves evaluating a combination of key performance indicators (KPIs) across various aspects of operations, including productivity, quality, on-time delivery, cycletime, efficiency, cost management, employee satisfaction and many others. Below is a comprehensive list to measure factory success:

- Productivity measures how efficiently a factory converts inputs (e.g., labor, materials, and energy) into outputs (e.g., finished goods).
- Overall Equipment Effectiveness (OEE) measures the efficiency of machinery and equipment.
- Production Output is the total quantity of goods produced in a given period (e.g., units per day, week, or month).
- Labor Productivity is the output per employee or labor hour.
- Quality metrics assess the ability of the factory to produce goods that meet specifications and customer expectations.
- Yield measures percentage of products that meet quality standards at output.
- Customer satisfaction
- Efficiency evaluates how well resources are utilized in the factory.
- Cycle Time is the time taken to complete one production cycle (from start to finish).
- Throughput rates at which products are produced (e.g., units per hour).
- Downtime measures the total time equipment or production lines are non-operational.
- Cost metrics track the financial performance of the factory. It includes cost per unit, scrap and rework costs,
- Inventory Turnover Ratio measures how quickly inventory is used and replaced.
- Delivery Metrics evaluate the factory's ability to meet customer demand on time, including On-Time Delivery (OTD), Lead Time, etc.

- Safety metrics assess the factory's commitment to maintaining a safe working environment.

By tracking these metrics and taking corrective actions, factories can achieve operational excellence, improve profitability, and maintain a competitive edge. One can also see how a particular automation system/ platform improves these metrics.

These metrics are measured by the data collected from the factory floor. Their reports serve as a guide line for the management of the factory.

Section 3.02   Industrial Robots

In the realm of modern factory automation, industrial robots have emerged as indispensable assets, revolutionizing manufacturing processes and significantly enhancing efficiency. Robotics can skillfully perform a diverse array of tasks across various industries. They are crucial in handling activities that are repetitive, hazardous, or demand a high degree of precision or handling heavy objects.

There are many kinds of industrial robots for different applications. The most common types of Industrial Robotics are:

- Articulated robots, featuring a human-like structure with multiple joints, are pivotal in diverse industries. The flexibility of these industrial robots allows precise movements, making them ideal for tasks like welding and assembly.
- SCARA robots, known for their selective compliance assembly arm, excel in high-speed, precision applications. With parallel rotary joints for horizontal movement, they are industrial robotics that are commonly used in assembly lines, especially in electronics and pharmaceutical manufacturing.

- Delta robots, characterized by three arms with parallel linkages, deliver rapid and precise movements in three dimensions. Widely used in tasks requiring high-speed performance, such as pick-and-place operations, these industrial robotics tend to enhance efficiency in packaging and food processing industries.

Section 3.03   Programmable Logic Controller (PLC)

A Programmable Logic Controller (PLC) is a specialized industrial computer used to control and automate manufacturing processes, machinery, and other industrial systems.

PLCs are widely used in industries such as automotive, food and beverage, pharmaceuticals, oil and gas, assembly lines in the robotic control, quality inspection and process control systems. They are designed to withstand harsh industrial environments and provide reliable, real-time control of complex processes.

It has modular designs, allowing users to add or remove input/output (I/O) modules, communication modules, and other components as needed.

PLCs operates in real-time to process inputs and generate outputs in real time, ensuring precise control of industrial processes.

PLCs can be programmed using various languages, such as Ladder Logic, Structured Text, Function Block Diagram (FBD), and Instruction List (IL).

PLCs usually integrate with other industrial automation systems and devices, such as SCADA (Supervisory Control and Data Acquisition) system, HMIs (Human-Machine Interfaces), sensors, actuators, and IoT platforms.

PLCs are increasingly being integrated with IoT platforms for remote monitoring and predictive maintenance.

As Edge Computing proliferates, PLCs with edge computing capabilities can process data locally, reducing latency and improving efficiency.

In doing so, PLC's are incorporating AI and Machine Learning for advanced process optimization and decision-making.

PLCs are considered as the basic component of industrial automation, providing reliable and flexible control for a wide range of applications.

Section 3.04 Human Machine Interface

All systems need to interface with human. Human-Machine Interface (HMI) or Human Machine Interaction Platform is the only communication interface between human and the physical-cyber world. It is a critical component of modern industrial and technological systems.

HMI's enable users to monitor, control, and optimize complex processes by providing intuitive visualizations, real-time data, and control capabilities. From manufacturing plants and energy systems to smart homes and consumer electronics. HMIs are ubiquitous, playing a vital role in enhancing efficiency, safety, and user experience. As technology continues to evolve, HMIs are becoming more sophisticated, incorporating advanced features such as touch screens, voice control, and augmented reality.

In industrial settings, HMIs are integral part to the Supervisory Control and Data Acquisition (SCADA) systems and Programmable Logic Controllers (PLCs). They provide operators with a graphical representation of processes, equipment status, and key performance indicators (KPIs). This allows operators to make informed decisions, troubleshoot issues, and optimize operations in real time. For example, in a manufacturing plant, an HMI might display the status of production lines, temperature readings, and machine alarms, enabling operators to intervene quickly in case of anomalies.

HMIs feature user-friendly interfaces with clear graphics, icons, and navigation menus. This reduces the learning curve for operators and minimizes the risk of errors. HMIs provide real-time data in the form of charts, graphs, and dashboards, allowing users to monitor processes and performance at a glance.

HMIs generate alerts and notifications to inform operators of critical events, such as equipment failures or process deviations. This ensures timely intervention and minimizes downtime.

Many HMIs now support remote access, allowing operators to monitor and control systems from anywhere using smartphones, tablets, or computers. This is particularly useful for managing distributed operations.

Advancements in technology, such as artificial intelligence (AI), augmented reality (AR), and the Internet of Things (IoT) will further enhance its capability. These innovations are enabling more intuitive, immersive, and intelligent interfaces. For example, AR-based HMIs can overlay digital information onto physical equipment, providing operators with real-time guidance and insights. In the last chapter, we will discuss the new features of HMI which integrated AI technologies such as Natural Language Processing capability.

Section 3.05   Distributed Control System (DCS)

Distributed Control System (DCS) is a computerized control system used to manage and control complex industrial processes or machinery across multiple locations. It is commonly employed in industries such as manufacturing, power generation, chemical processing, oil and gas, and water treatment.

The key feature of a DCS is its decentralized architecture, where control functions are distributed across multiple controllers or nodes, rather than being centralized in a single unit.

In DCS, control functions are spread across multiple controllers or nodes, which are connected via a communication network. Each controller handles a specific part of the process, allowing for localized control and reducing the risk of system-wide failures.

DCS systems often have built-in redundant components to ensure high reliability and availability.

DCS systems can be easily expanded by adding more controllers or nodes to accommodate larger or more complex processes.

DCS systems operate in real-time, ensuring timely monitoring and control of industrial processes. And they are integrated with other systems, such as Supervisory Control and Data Acquisition (SCADA) systems, Enterprise Resource Planning (ERP) systems, and Manufacturing Execution Systems (MES).

There are many components and installations, such as control valves, pumps, motors, and heaters, to allow process parameters adjustment based on signals from the control system.

DCS systems typically include a centralized operator interface, often in the form of a Human-Machine Interface (HMI), which allows operators to monitor and control the entire process from a single location.

DCS has many built-in components such as controllers, Input/Output (I/O) Modules, communication Network, Human-Machine Interface (HMI) such as operator stations, engineering stations. HMI provides operators and engineers with real-time data and control options through graphical interfaces for monitoring and control as well as troubleshooting.

DCS also contains a huge historical database. This database is the heart of Advanced Process Control (APC). APC uses algorithms and models to optimize process performance. Increasingly, APC is more and more integrated into the Edge and Cloud computing using AI for real-time and more precise process control. Examples are Model Predictive Control (MPC), real-time optimization (RTO).

Section 3.06   Model Predictive Control (MPC)

Model Predictive Control (MPC) is an advanced control strategy used in process control and automation to optimize the performance of dynamic systems. It is widely used in industries such as chemical processing, oil and gas, power generation, automotive, and robotics. MPC is particularly effective for systems with complex dynamics, constraints, and multiple inputs and outputs (MIMO).

As the name implies, MPC has a predictive mathematical model. MPC can predict the future behavior of the system over a finite time horizon based on current and past inputs, outputs, and disturbances.

At each control interval, MPC solves an optimization problem to determine the best sequence of control actions (inputs) that minimize a cost function while satisfying system constraints.

MPC uses a "receding horizon" approach. Only the first control action in the optimized sequence is applied to the system. At the next time step, the process is repeated with updated measurements, ensuring continuous adaptation to changing conditions. MPC explicitly handles constraints on inputs (e.g., actuator limits), outputs (e.g., safety limits), and states (e.g., physical limits). This makes it highly suitable for real-world applications where constraints are critical.

MPC incorporates feedback by using real-time measurements to update the predictions and optimize control actions, ensuring robustness to uncertainties and disturbances.

MPC model is built with state-space equations, transfer functions, or empirical models and it is dynamic. This model describes how the system responds to inputs and disturbances. It can do control and optimization.

Using the model, MPC predicts the future behavior of the system over a finite prediction horizon (e.g., the next 10–20 time steps).

A cost function is defined to quantify the control objectives, such as minimizing tracking error, reducing energy consumption, or maintaining safe operating conditions.

MPC solves an optimization problem to find the sequence of control actions that minimizes the cost function while satisfying constraints. This is typically done using numerical optimization techniques.

The first control action in the optimized sequence is applied to the system. The rest of the sequence is discarded. At the next time step, the process is repeated with updated measurements, ensuring continuous adaptation to changes in the system or environment.

MPC explicitly accounts for constraints on inputs, outputs, and states, making it ideal for real-world applications. MPC can handle systems with multiple inputs and outputs, making it suitable for complex processes.

By minimizing a cost function, MPC ensures optimal performance with respect to the defined objectives. MPC can handle uncertainties and disturbances by incorporating feedback and updating predictions in real-time. MPC can be tailored to specific applications by adjusting the prediction horizon, cost function, and constraints.

MPC is extensively used in chemical processes from controlling reactors, distillation columns, to the polymerization processes.

Consider a temperature control system for a chemical reactor: A dynamic model predicts how the reactor temperature changes based on heating input and external disturbances.

At any given time, MPC predicts the future temperature trajectory. It calculates the optimal sequence of heater inputs to minimize energy use while keeping the temperature on target.

In the oil and gas industry, it optimizes drilling, refining, and pipeline operations. In the power systems, it managing grid stability, load balancing, and renewable energy integration.

Model Predictive Control (MPC) is a powerful and versatile control strategy that combines prediction, optimization, and feedback to achieve optimal performance in complex systems. Its ability to handle constraints and multivariable systems makes it a preferred choice for many industrial applications.

By leveraging automation, chemical plants can achieve higher productivity, better product quality, and safer operations in continuous processes.

Section 3.07   SCADA

Supervisory Control and Data Acquisition (SCADA) is a powerful hardware-software integrated system used to monitor, control, and optimize industrial processes across various sectors, including manufacturing, energy, water treatment, and transportation.

SCADA systems provide real-time data acquisition, visualization, and control capabilities, enabling operators to manage complex processes efficiently and respond quickly to changing conditions.

The hardware of a SCADA system consists Remote Terminal Units (RTUs) and Programmable Logic Controllers (PLCs). These devices are deployed at remote sites to collect data from sensors and equipment. RTUs and PLCs execute control commands and transmit data to the central SCADA system.

With RTU's, operators can remotely control equipment and processes, reducing the need for on-site intervention and improving operational efficiency.

In addition to RTU's, SCADA also has a central monitoring station, where data from all remote sites is aggregated and analyzed. Operators can issue commands, adjust parameters, and respond to alerts from this central location.

The advanced Human-Machine Interface (HMI) allows operators to interact with the SCADA system. It provides real-time visualizations of processes, alarms, and trends, enabling operators to monitor and control operations effectively.

SCADA systems rely on communication networks (e.g., wired, wireless, or fiber-optic) to transmit data between field devices, control centers, and the central system. Reliable communication is essential for ensuring seamless operation.

SCADA software is responsible for data processing, analysis, and storage. It also generates reports, triggers alarms, and supports decision-making.

SCADA system provides real-time monitoring, data logging. All historical data are stored in a centralized server or cloud/ edge, which can be used for trend analysis, performance evaluation, and compliance reporting. Alarms are generated when there is an equipment failures or process deviations to alert operators to take necessary actions.

SCADA systems do not work along in the factory. They can integrate with other enterprise systems, such as Enterprise Resource Planning (ERP) and Manufacturing Execution Systems (MES), to provide a holistic view of operations.

With access to real-time and historical data, operators and managers can make informed decisions to improve processes and achieve business goals.

Section 3.08   Operational Technology (OT)

Operational Technology (OT) refers to the hardware and software systems used to monitor, control, and manage physical devices, processes, and infrastructure in industrial environments.

Unlike Information Technology (IT), which focuses on data processing and communication, OT is primarily concerned with the direct control and operation of industrial equipment and systems. OT is the backbone of industries such as manufacturing, energy, utilities, transportation, and healthcare, enabling the automation and optimization of complex processes.

OT systems are designed to perform critical functions in industrial settings, including:

- Monitoring: Collecting real-time data from sensors and devices to track the performance of equipment and processes.

- Control: Executing commands to manage machinery, production lines, and other physical assets.
- Automation: Reducing human intervention by automating repetitive or hazardous tasks.
- Safety: Ensuring the safe operation of equipment and processes, often through fail-safes and emergency shutdown systems.

OT systems consist of several key components that work together to achieve these functions. We have discussed all of them in the previous chapters. They include SCADA, Distributed Control Systems (DCS), PLCs, Industrial Robotics, Sensors and Actuators.

The advent of Industry 4.0 and the Industrial Internet of Things (IIoT) has transformed the role of OT. Traditionally, OT systems operated in isolation, with limited connectivity to IT networks. However, the integration of OT and IT is now driving the next wave of industrial innovation. This convergence enables Data-Driven Decision Making, Predictive Maintenance, Smart Manufacturing, and many others.

In conclusion, OT is the foundation of industrial automation, enabling the control and optimization of physical processes. As industries continue to embrace digital transformation, the convergence of OT and IT will play a pivotal role in driving innovation, efficiency, and sustainability. By addressing the challenges and leveraging the opportunities, companies can unlock the full potential of OT in the era of Industry 4.0.

Section 3.09   WIP Transport Systems

Factory floor needs to move large amount of production materials, whether Work-In-Progress (WIP), or raw materials and spare parts for equipment from one location to the other. Without automation, huge amount of manpower needs to do the job.

WIP transport systems are mechanisms or processes used to move partially completed products or raw materials between different stages of production within a manufacturing or assembly environment. They are necessary because they can reduce the lead times of delivering WIP's, therefore, lowering inventory costs, and speed up production by improved production flow and reduced bottlenecks. When transporting heavy items, such as auto parts, they also enhanced worker productivity and safety.

Efficient WIP transport systems are critical for maintaining smooth workflows, reducing bottlenecks, and optimizing production efficiency.

There are many kinds of WIP transport systems, suitable for different types of factories. Some of the most common ones are discussed in this section.

Conveyor Systems have been used in the industry for many decades. There are different types of the conveyors: Belt Conveyors are used for transporting lightweight to medium-weight items. Roller Conveyors are ideal for moving heavy or bulky items. Overhead Conveyors are suspended systems for transporting items through the air, saving floor space. Chain Conveyors are suitable for heavy-duty applications, such as automotive assembly lines.

Automated Guided Vehicles (AGVs) is a newer type of transport system in the factory. They are driverless vehicles equipped with sensors and navigation systems that enable them to navigate predefined paths within a facility. These vehicles efficiently transport materials, components, or finished products from one point to another, minimizing the need for manual intervention in material handling processes.

There are various types of AGVs, designed for specific functions such as material transport, pallet handling, or assembly line support between workstations or storage areas. They normally follow predefined paths (e.g., magnetic strips, lasers, or vision systems). Examples are Forklift AGVs, unit-load AGVs.

These robotic vehicles not only optimize logistical workflows but also contribute to a safer working environment by reducing the risk of accidents associated with these manual tasks.

There are also Autonomous Mobile Robots (AMRs), which are more advanced than AGVs, AMRs use sensors and AI to navigate dynamically. They can adapt to changes in the environment and optimize routes in real-time.

Pneumatic or Vacuum Transport Systems are used for moving lightweight or granular materials through tubes using air pressure or vacuum. They are common in industries like food processing or pharmaceuticals.

Sortation Systems automatically sort items based on size, weight, destination, or other criteria. Examples include tilt-tray sorters and cross-belt sorters. Post office and UPS use sortation systems to sort and route mail, packages to their correct destinations.

In the warehouse, Automated Storage and Retrieval Systems (AS/RS) are computer-controlled systems for automatically placing and retrieving loads from defined storage locations. They include vertical lift modules, carousels, and unit-load systems.

Important considerations for choosing a WIP transport system for a factory depend many factors, such as throughput requirements, flexibility, space utilization and cost. Sometimes, a factory may adapt more than one type of WIP transport systems.

Since the WIP transport systems are not working along, they must be compatible with the existing production systems and software (e.g., ERP or MES).

By selecting the right WIP transport system, manufacturers can significantly improve their operational efficiency and competitiveness.

Chapter IV. Factory Automation II – Platforms and Systems

In this chapter, we will discuss platforms and systems in the factory automation. In general, platform is foundation or environment where different applications, services, or processes can operate. While, system is composed of self-contained, interconnected components working together to achieve a specific purpose. However, these two concepts are sometimes used interchangeably. Both platforms and systems are built from the components discussed in the previous chapter.

For different aspects of the operation performance, different platforms and systems are used to control and optimize. The most important ones are:

MES (Manufacturing Execution System)
ERP (Enterprise Resource Planning System)
QMS (Quality Management System)
SMS (Supply Chain Management System)
SPC (Statistical Process Control)·
APC (Automatic Process Control)
YMS (Yield Management System)
SCADA (Supervisory Control and Data Acquisition)
HMI (Human Machine Interface)
CAD and CAM (Computer Aided Design and Computer Aided Manufacturing)
DFM (Design for Manufacturability)
WMS (Warehouse Management System)
PMS (Predictive Maintenance Software)
APS (Advance Production Scheduling)

Section 4.01   Manufacturing Execution System

Manufacturing Execution System (MES) is a digital framework that serves as the central nervous system of modern manufacturing. It is a factory floor management system. It connects enterprise-level planning (e.g., ERP systems) with real-time shop floor operations, ensuring that manufacturing operations are executed efficiently and in alignment with business goals.

It monitors, controls, and optimizes every aspects of the production processes, ensuring efficiency, quality, and compliance. For example, it records the locations and process steps of every lots of WIP in the production line, the equipment or workstation that the lot is being processed, its process parameters recorded and reported by the sensors in the equipment, the physical location of a lot in the factory, whether the lot is being transported or in the queue in front of a workstation, or being processed. It knows the status of each equipment or workstation, whether it is in production, under maintenance or idling.

By acting as a bridge between the production goals and execution, MES is indispensable in industries ranging from automotive and aerospace to pharmaceuticals, food production and semiconductor wafer fab.

It is a software-based solution used in manufacturing to monitor, track, and control the production process in real time. MES provides visibility into the production process, enabling manufacturers to optimize workflows, improve quality, and reduce costs.

MES provides a supervisory function of most of the systems and platforms in the factory. Systems, such as ERP, QMS, SMS, SPC, APC, YMS, WMS, PMS, APS, either work under the supervision of MES or attached to MES to serve as an interface between MES and other business automation systems.

To perform the job, MES collects data directly from machines, sensors, and workers to track the status of production lines, equipment performance, and workflow progress. Dashboards display metrics like cycle times, downtime causes, and Overall Equipment Effectiveness (OEE).

MES also translates high-level production plans from ERP into actionable work orders. It schedules tasks, allocates resources (materials, labor, tools), and ensures the right instructions reach operators at the right time.

MES enforces quality standards through the QMS. It triggers corrective actions, documents deviations, and ensures compliance with regulations.

From raw materials to finished goods, MES tracks every component's journey. This end-to-end traceability is critical for recalls, audits, and sustainability reporting.

Advanced analytics identify bottlenecks, predict maintenance needs, and optimize workflows. For example, AI-powered MES might recommend adjusting machine parameters to reduce energy consumption.

Different industries require different setups for MES. For example, in the automotive industry, MES tracks thousands of components in assembly lines to ensure just-in-time delivery. In the pharmaceutical industry, it monitors sterile environments and batch processes to comply with Good Manufacturing Practices (GMP). In the food & beverage, it manages expiry dates, allergen controls, and lot tracking.

As Industry 4.0 accelerates, MES is evolving into a more intelligent, interconnected system. As AI and machine learning evolve, MES acquires capability of predictive analytics for demand forecasting and autonomous decision-making. Virtual replicas of production lines simulate scenarios to optimize outcomes.

Cloud-based MES enables remote monitoring and scalability for global operations. Cloud-based MES becomes indispensable for the companies with multiple manufacturing sites, which require integrated operation. Edge computing processes data locally for faster response times in critical processes.

A Manufacturing Execution System is the backbone of smart manufacturing, transforming raw data into actionable insights. By harmonizing planning, execution, and analysis, MES empowers manufacturers to meet the demands of a competitive, fast-paced market.

As technologies like AI and IoT mature, MES will continue to drive innovation, enabling factories to operate with unprecedented precision, flexibility, and sustainability. For businesses aiming to thrive in the Fourth Industrial Revolution, investing in a robust MES is no longer optional—it's essential.

Almost all industries used MES. Examples are automotive, aerospace, pharmaceuticals, food and beverage, electronics, semiconductor, chemicals , consumer goods and others.

By implementing an MES, manufacturers can achieve greater operational efficiency, improved product quality, and better overall control of their production processes. It is safe to say that today's factory cannot function without MES.

Section 4.02   Automatic Materials Handling System

A more sophisticated kind of the transport system is called the Automatic Materials Handling System (AMHS). It is a combination of equipment, software, and controls designed to automate the movement, storage, and retrieval of materials in a manufacturing, warehouse, or distribution environment. These systems are widely used in industries such as automotive, electronics, pharmaceuticals, and logistics to improve efficiency, reduce labor costs, and enhance accuracy.

AMHS is composed of many subsystems. It has a central control system, which is a software and hardware platform that manage and coordinate the operation of the AMHS. It also interfaces with warehouse management systems (WMS), and enterprise resource planning (ERP) integration.

AMHS also includes storage systems, such as automated racks, shelves, and bins for storing materials. The storage systems are often integrated with AS/RS for efficient space utilization.

AMHS operates using many sensors and IoT devices. WIP containers are equipped with RFID. RFID readers are installed all over AMHS and workstations so that the WIP locations are being tracked all the time through the IoT-enabled devices for real-time data collection and analysis in the centralized server in the MES.

AMHS is a key component of factory automation. They enable manufacturers to handle large volumes of materials with minimal manual labor. AMHS also interface with the AS/RS in the warehouse to automatically retrieve and deliver items to the production line, reducing the time and effort required for manual picking.

By implementing an AMHS, factory can achieve greater operational efficiency, reduce costs, and improve customer satisfaction through faster and more accurate order fulfillment.

Section 4.03   Warehouse Management System

A Warehouse Management System (WMS) is a software solution designed to streamline and optimize the operations of a warehouse or distribution center. It provides tools and functionalities to manage inventory, track goods, and coordinate workflows, ensuring that products are stored, picked, packed, and shipped efficiently. In today's fast-paced and highly competitive supply chain environment, a WMS is essential for businesses seeking to improve accuracy, reduce costs, and enhance customer satisfaction. By leveraging real-time data and automation, WMS solutions enable organizations to maximize the efficiency of their warehouse operations.

WMS automates a wide range of functions to support warehouse operations. One of its major function is the inventory management.   A WMS provides real-time visibility into inventory levels, locations, and movements. It helps businesses track stock accurately, reduce overstocking or stockouts, and optimize storage space.

The WMS system streamlines the order fulfillment process by automating tasks such as picking, packing, and shipping. It ensures that orders are processed quickly and accurately, improving customer satisfaction. It simplifies the receiving process by automating the recording of incoming goods and directing them to the optimal storage locations. This reduces handling time and minimizes errors. It also uses algorithms to determine the most efficient picking routes and methods, such as batch picking or zone picking. This reduces travel time and increases productivity.

In addition, a WMS coordinates the shipping process by generating packing lists, labels, and shipping documents. It also integrates with carriers to ensure timely and cost-effective deliveries. It provides detailed reports and analytics on warehouse performance, including metrics such as order accuracy, inventory turnover, and labor productivity. These insights help businesses identify areas for improvement.

More and more, artificial intelligence (AI), robotics, and the Internet of Things (IoT) are integrated into WMS. These innovations are enabling more intelligent and automated warehouse operations. For example, AI-powered WMS solutions can predict demand, optimize inventory levels, and recommend efficient picking routes. Similarly, IoT-enabled devices, such as smart shelves and automated guided vehicles (AGVs), are enhancing the capabilities of WMS by providing real-time data and automating physical tasks.

As technology continues to advance, WMS solutions will become even more sophisticated, offering new possibilities for automation and optimization in warehouse management.

Section 4.04   Supply Chain Management System

Supply Chain Management System (SCMS) is a software module attached to MES to manage the flow of goods, services, information, and finances across the entire supply chain—from raw material suppliers to manufacturers, distributors, retailers, and ultimately, the end customer. It uses the data collected from the factory and stored in the MES server. It helps factory optimize their supply chain operations, reduce costs, improve efficiency, and enhance customer satisfaction.

In a factory, the SCMS interfaces with the systems in the business side. It performs several important functions in the factory.

First is the planning function. It performs demand forecasting, inventory planning, and production scheduling. In the production scheduling, it takes into account the current factory capacity, production loading, promised delivery date of the finished products. It ensures the right products are available at the right time and place. Any inconsistency will be notified to the business side to take actions. For example, if the factory loading is too high, it may slow down loading new lots into the production line.

At the same time, it manages procurement of raw materials; supplier relationships monitor supplier performance, and process purchase orders.

It also tracks stock levels, manages warehouse operations, and optimizes inventory turnover, manages to reduce carrying costs and prevents stock outs or overstocking.

On the factory floor, it manages production processes, work orders, and quality control from the point of view of materials supply. For example, it has procedures to ensure that every delivery of raw materials meets the quality standards.

It also manages the movement of goods, including shipping, routing, and tracking. It processes customer orders, manages order status, and ensures on-time delivery.

Warehouse management is also under the SCMS. It includes the raw materials warehouse as well as finished goods warehouse. Automation in the warehouse includes robotics and automation in warehouses and logistics.

By implementing a Supply Chain Management System, organizations can achieve greater operational efficiency, reduce costs, and improve customer satisfaction, ultimately gaining a competitive edge in their industry.

Section 4.05   Quality Management System

Quality management System (QMS) is a module attached to the MES to handle all the quality related data and issues. It monitors and controls product quality during production. It tracks defects, deviations, and compliance with standards.

Quality Management System (QMS) is a formalized system that documents processes, procedures, and responsibilities for achieving quality policies and objectives. It helps organizations coordinate and direct activities to meet customer and regulatory requirements while improving efficiency and effectiveness. A well-implemented QMS ensures consistent quality in products or services, enhances customer satisfaction, and drives continuous improvement.

QMS includes Quality Policy and Objectives, a statement of the organization's commitment to quality. It contains specific, measurable objectives aligned with the quality policy. An expanded QMS is called Total Quality Management (TQM). It is a holistic approach to quality that involves all employees in continuous improvement.

A good quality management system starts with control of the quality of workflow. The workflow procedure is carefully documented and stored in the document control. The document control procedure is strictly controlled by the algorithm in the QMS module. It regulates how documents (e.g., procedures, work instructions, policies) are approved, updated, and accessible to relevant personnel. These documents are the basis of all operations in the factory.

QMS also contains tools like PDCA (Plan-Do-Check-Act) and Kaizen to sustain the ongoing efforts to improve processes, products, and services. Other tools include Process Mapping for visual representation of workflows to identify inefficiencies, Root Cause Analysis techniques such as 5 Whys and Fishbone Diagram (Ishikawa) to identify the source of problems, etc.

The standards and frameworks for QMS are heavily regulated by ISO 9001, a worldwide standard for QMS. Customers always want to know whether a factory is certified by ISO 9001 or not. For different industries, different QMS standards apply:

- ISO 13485: QMS for medical devices.
- IATF 16949: QMS for the automotive industry.
- AS9100: QMS for aerospace.
- ISO 22000: QMS for food safety.

QMS provides a framework for organizations to ensure consistent quality and continuous improvement.

By integrating QMS into MES, it can be ensured that the operation cannot continue if QMS standards are not met.

By implementing a QMS, factory can achieve operational excellence, meet customer expectations, and maintain a competitive edge in their industry.

Section 4.06   Document Control

Document control has an extremely important function in controlling all regulated documents in the factory. It is the legal frame work of the business workflow.

The basis of operation and workflow are all documented. The procedures must follow the predefined rules, which are specified in the documents. No one can change these rules without predefined approval procedure. For example, a process recipe for a given process flow has a version upgrade to correct a defect in the process, the updated version has to be used in the production involving specific equipment and specific product. And this is clearly specified in the document.

In fact, ISO 9001, places significant emphasis on document control as a critical component of a Quality Management System (QMS). Document control ensures that organizations maintain, update, and distribute documents in a systematic way to ensure consistency, accuracy, and compliance with quality standards.

ISO 9001 outlines the requirements for documented information, which includes both document control and record control. It requires organizations to establish and maintain a documented procedure to ensure documents are reviewed and approved for suitability and accuracy before use, to periodically review documents and update them as necessary to ensure they remain relevant and effective, to track changes to documents and clearly indicate the revision status (e.g., version control), and to make sure that the correct and up-to-date versions of documents are accessible to those who need them.

Section 4.07   Automatic Production Scheduling

Advanced Production Scheduling (APS) is a sophisticated approach to planning and managing manufacturing operations, designed to optimize resource utilization, minimize production lead times, and improve overall efficiency.

In today's fast-paced and highly competitive manufacturing environment, APS has become an essential tool for companies seeking to meet customer demands, reduce costs, and maintain a competitive edge. By leveraging advanced algorithms, real-time data, and integration with other enterprise systems, APS enables manufacturers to create more accurate, flexible, and responsive production schedules.

Traditional production scheduling methods often rely on manual processes or simple software tools, which can struggle to handle the complexity and variability of modern manufacturing environments. Factors such as machine breakdowns, material shortages, and changing customer demands and priorities can disrupt production plans, leading to inefficiencies, delays, and increased costs. Advanced Production Scheduling addresses these challenges by providing a dynamic and data-driven approach to scheduling that can adapt to changing conditions in real time.

APS integrates with other enterprise systems, such as Enterprise Resource Planning (ERP), Manufacturing Execution Systems (MES), and supply chain management tools, to access real-time data on inventory levels, machine availability, workforce capacity, and customer orders. This ensures that schedules are based on the most up-to-date information.

APS uses advanced algorithms to evaluate multiple scheduling scenarios and identify the most efficient plan. These algorithms consider constraints such as machine capacity, labor availability, material requirements, and delivery deadlines to create an optimized schedule that minimizes waste and maximizes throughput.

APS systems allow manufacturers to simulate different scenarios and assess the impact of potential changes, such as adding a new order, delaying a shipment, or experiencing a machine breakdown. This capability enables proactive decision-making and helps mitigate risks.

APS provides intuitive dashboards and Gantt charts that visualize production schedules, making it easier for planners and managers to understand and adjust plans as needed. This enhances communication and collaboration across teams.

Many APS systems incorporate automation and artificial intelligence (AI) to streamline scheduling processes. For example, AI can predict potential bottlenecks or recommend optimal sequencing of jobs based on historical data and trends.

By using APS, factory can optimize resource allocation and minimizing downtime, APS helps manufacturers achieve higher levels of productivity and efficiency. APS enables faster response to customer orders by streamlining production processes and reducing delays, leading to shorter lead times and improved customer satisfaction. By minimizing waste, reducing inventory levels, and avoiding rush orders, APS helps manufacturers lower operational costs and improve profitability.

APS allows manufacturers to quickly adapt to changes in demand, supply chain disruptions, or production issues, ensuring that schedules remain aligned with business goals.

With access to real-time data and advanced analytics, manufacturers can make more informed decisions about production planning, resource allocation, and capacity management.

Advanced Production Scheduling is a transformative tool for modern manufacturing, enabling companies to optimize their operations, respond to market demands, and stay competitive in an increasingly dynamic environment. By leveraging real-time data, advanced algorithms, and automation, APS empowers manufacturers to create more efficient, flexible, and resilient production schedules. As industries continue to evolve, APS will play an increasingly critical role in driving operational excellence and sustainable growth.

Section 4.08   Line Balance and Inventory Turn Management

Line balance refers to the even distribution of WIP, thus the task of production, at every workstation and equipment on the factory floor. The perfectly balanced line is a ideal situation of the production line- All WIP's on the factory floor are evenly distributed among equipment and workstations. There is no bottleneck and congestion. It represents the maximum WIP flow, therefore, the maximum productivity. Perfect balanced line has maximum throughput, minimum equipment idle time, lower production costs, improved workflow, and shortest cycletime.

When the line is unbalanced, some workstations become bottlenecks and pile up huge WIP queue, while other workstations stay idle for the lack of WIP. The purpose of balancing a line is to relieve or even avoid such situation.

Line Balancing in a factory is a production strategy to achieve the uniform distribution of the production tasks over each workstation in the proper balance of the resources. The goal is to ensure that each workstation has an equal amount of work, minimizing idle time, bottlenecks, and overburdening of resources. This optimization leads to increased efficiency, reduced production costs, and improved throughput.

In the real situation, the line is never truly balanced, because there are always disturbances, which causes WIP to distribute unevenly. For example, equipment down event can cause the WIP piling up. Or change of product mix in the production line changes the use of equipment in different proportion. In many cases, worker skill levels and fatigue can impact task performance. For example, a less experienced engineer may take longer to repair a machine. There are many other factors that can cause disturbance in the line balance.

Therefore, line balancing is a continuous effort to resolve the disturbance, remove the bottleneck and bring the line into balance again. To do so, it requires strategies.

Each equipment and workstation have different throughput. Some works faster than the others. Naturally, the equipment which works faster can take more WIP. Therefore, the ratio of throughput to the WIP in front of the equipment is the ideal parameter to monitor the line balance. This ratio is called the WIP turn. WIP turn can be applied to the individual equipment. It can also be applied to a group of similar equipment, or even to the entire factory. It can be used for a particular product in the line.

Inventory turn is a direct consequence of the line balance. Factory automation also plays a crucial role in improving inventory turn. Automated systems can track inventory levels in real time and generate alerts when stock levels fall below a certain threshold. This enables manufacturers to replenish inventory promptly, reducing the risk of stock outs and overstocking. Additionally, automated systems can optimize the layout of the warehouse to minimize the time required to locate and retrieve items, further improving inventory turnover.

The number of products processed by the equipment is known as "moves". This WIP turn is the turn rate of WIP inventory at the equipment: number of moves divided by average WIP queue for a given period of time, say 24 hours.

By listing the inventory turns of all equipment, we will be able to see the distribution of WIP turn around average WIP turn. The average deviation, or sigma, indicates the line balance. When the deviation is larger, the line balance is worse.

If an equipment processed 2,000 products in a given day with average queue of WIP queue in front of the equipment being 200, the WIP turn is 2,000/200=10.

WIP turn is inversely proportional to the cycletime. For the entire factory, if the WIP turn is at 10, and the production process has 500 steps, the cycletime is therefore 500 steps/ 10 steps per day, or 50 days.

When we improve WIP turn, the cycletime improves. When the average time WIP stays in the factory becomes shorter, the total WIP goes down for a fixed product start rate. Therefore, we can say that the productivity or efficiency of the factory increases.

To optimize line balance, factory needs to collect throughput and WIP queue data from each piece of equipment throughout the factory. Such data determine the deviation of line balance.

Actions need to be taken to bring the areas or equipment with smallest WIP turn to the factory average. This can be done by improving the throughput and/ or reducing the WIP queue.

If the equipment is down, its capacity is reduced. Maintenance needs to bring the equipment back to production as soon as possible. Otherwise, WIP will start to accumulate in front of the equipment. The WIP turn goes down.

Since there are many equipment in the factory that can be down at any given time, by assigning priority to the equipment with lowest WIP turn can have better impact to the performance of factory.

Another way to reduce the WIP queue in the equipment is to dispatch WIP away from the non-performing equipment, using dispatching software. It redirects the WIP traffic to lessen the congestion. The WIP is routed in preferential to the workstations with high WIP turn.

There are many other techniques for line balancing, such as heuristic method or using mathematics models. The heuristic line balancing uses rules of thumb or practical strategies to find a good, though not necessarily optimal, solution.

Common Heuristic Methods include Largest Candidate Rule (LCR), Kilbridge and Wester Method, Ranked Positional Weight (RPW) Method, COMSOAL (Computer Method for Sequencing Operations for Assembly

Lines), etc. The goal is to achieve a balanced line where each workstation has a similar amount of work, minimizing idle time and maximizing throughput. These methods are particularly useful when dealing with complex problems where finding an exact solution is computationally intensive or impractical.

Today, with the advancement of AI and digital twin, it is feasible to simulate the actions using different balancing techniques to find the best result for optimization.

By effectively balancing the production line, factories can achieve higher productivity, reduce waste, and meet customer demand more efficiently. Line balancing is a complicated task. It must be done by automation.

Line balancing is a critical aspect of factory automation. It involves distributing tasks evenly across workstations to ensure a smooth and efficient production flow. Automated systems can monitor the workload at each station and adjust the flow of materials accordingly. For example, if one workstation is operating slower than others, the system can reroute materials to prevent bottlenecks. This ensures that the production line operates at maximum efficiency.

Section 4.09   Dispatching System

A dispatching system in a factory is a critical component of production management, responsible for coordinating and allocating resources, tasks, and materials to ensure smooth and efficient operations. It is an important tool for line balance management. It acts as the central hub for decision-making on the shop floor, ensuring that the right tasks are assigned to the right resources at the right time. By optimizing workflow and minimizing delays, dispatching systems play a vital role in enhancing productivity, reducing costs, and meeting delivery deadlines.

Major functions of a Dispatching System are:

- Task Assignment: The system assigns tasks to machines, workstations, or operators based on predefined rules, priorities, and availability. For example, it might prioritize urgent orders or allocate tasks to machines with the shortest setup times.
- Resource Allocation: It ensures that resources such as raw materials, tools, and labor are available when and where they are needed. This prevents bottlenecks and idle time.
- Real-Time Monitoring: The system tracks the progress of tasks, machine status, and operator performance in real time. This allows for quick adjustments in case of delays or disruptions.
- Scheduling and Sequencing: Dispatching systems create optimized schedules for production tasks, considering factors like machine capacity, order deadlines, and material availability. They also sequence tasks to minimize changeover times and maximize throughput.
- Communication and Coordination: The system acts as a communication bridge between different departments (e.g., production, inventory, and maintenance) to ensure seamless coordination.

In the factory without automation, dispatching is done manually, usually the responsibility of the Department of Production Control. It relies on production control engineers to assign tasks and manage resources. While simple, it is prone to errors and inefficiencies, especially in complex environments.

In a semi-automated dispatching system, the dispatching is still done by the engineers but with the help of software tools to assist in task assignment and scheduling.

Now a days, fully automated dispatching uses advanced algorithms and real-time data to make decisions without human intervention. And it sends the dispatching actions to the factory floor through the relevant automation systems, such as AHMS, for the execution. This is ideal for high-volume, dynamic production environments.

As the name implies, dispatching system matches the available resources to the job demand in the optimized manner. Because many resources are needed to make a production task to happen, such as equipment, WIP, process, operator etc., and there are thousands of production tasks in progress at any given time, a dispatching system needs to have sophisticated algorithm to do the job.

A dispatching system is attached in the MES, and takes the data from the MES database for its algorithm to work. Its actions are executed by the WIP transport system. It is also integrated with the ERP systems, Inventory Management System, etc. for high-level production planning and inventory management.

A more advanced dispatch system can also be powered by AI and Machine Learning for predictive algorithms will optimize dispatching decisions by analyzing historical data and predicting future demand or disruptions. The system also depends on the connected machines and sensors to provide real-time data for more accurate dispatching.

Virtual replicas of the factory, known as the Digital Twin, will simulate dispatching scenarios to identify the most efficient workflows.

The dispatching system is the backbone of efficient factory operations, ensuring that resources are utilized effectively and production goals are met. By automating task assignment, resource allocation, and real-time monitoring, it eliminates inefficiencies and enhances productivity. As factories embrace Industry 4.0 technologies, dispatching systems will become even more intelligent, adaptive, and integral to achieving operational excellence. For manufacturers aiming to stay competitive in a fast-paced market, investing in a robust dispatching system is no longer a luxury—it's a necessity.

Section 4.10   Yield Management System

Yield Management System (YMS) is a dynamic pricing and inventory management tool used primarily in industries with perishable inventory and fixed capacity, such as hospitality, airlines, car rentals, and entertainment. The goal of a YMS is to maximize revenue by optimizing the price and allocation of available resources based on demand forecasts, market conditions, and customer behavior. By leveraging data analytics, algorithms, and real-time adjustments, yield management systems enable businesses to sell the right product to the right customer at the right time and price.

Yield management, also known as revenue management, originated in the airline industry in the 1980s as a response to the challenge of filling seats while maximizing revenue. Since then, it has been adopted by various industries where capacity is fixed, and demand fluctuates. The core principle of yield management is to balance supply and demand by adjusting prices and availability in real time. This ensures that businesses can capture the highest possible revenue from their limited resources.

YMS relies on accurate demand forecasting to predict future customer behavior. This involves analyzing historical data, market trends, seasonal patterns, and external factors such as economic conditions or special events. Advanced YMS solutions use machine learning and artificial intelligence to improve the accuracy of these forecasts.

Dynamic pricing is a cornerstone of yield management. Prices are adjusted in real time based on factors such as demand levels, booking patterns, competitor pricing, and remaining inventory. For example, airlines may increase ticket prices as the departure date approaches and seats become scarce, while hotels may offer discounts during low-demand periods to attract more guests.

YMS optimizes the allocation of available inventory (e.g., hotel rooms, airline seats, or rental cars) across different customer segments and distribution channels. This ensures that high-value customers are prioritized while still capturing revenue from price-sensitive customers.

YMS segment customers based on factors such as booking behavior, price sensitivity, and loyalty. This allows businesses to tailor pricing and marketing strategies to different customer groups, maximizing revenue from each segment.

YMS continuously monitors market conditions and adjusts pricing and inventory allocation in real time. This agility enables businesses to respond quickly to changes in demand or competitor actions.

By optimizing prices and inventory allocation, a YMS helps businesses capture the maximum revenue from their fixed capacity. This is particularly important in industries with high fixed costs and low variable costs.

YMS automates complex pricing and inventory decisions, reducing the need for manual intervention and minimizing the risk of human error. This improves operational efficiency and allows staff to focus on strategic tasks.

By offering the right product at the right price, a YMS can improve customer satisfaction and loyalty. For example, price-sensitive customers may appreciate last-minute discounts, while premium customers may value guaranteed availability.

Businesses that implement a YMS gain a competitive edge by responding more effectively to market dynamics and customer preferences. This can lead to increased market share and profitability.

YMS provides valuable insights into customer behavior, market trends, and pricing strategies. These insights enable businesses to make informed decisions and refine their revenue management strategies over time.

A Yield Management System is a powerful tool for businesses in industries with perishable inventory and fixed capacity. By optimizing pricing and inventory allocation, a YMS enables businesses to maximize revenue, improve efficiency, and enhance customer satisfaction. As technology continues to evolve, yield management systems will become even more sophisticated, leveraging AI and machine learning to deliver even greater value. For businesses looking to thrive in competitive markets, investing in a YMS is a strategic move that can drive long-term success.

Section 4.11   Statistical Process Control (SPC)

SPC is a module residing in the MES to analyze all data collected from the factory floor statistically. It is the first step to organize data in a meaningful way. By using statistical techniques, SPC helps identify variations in processes and determines whether they are within acceptable limits or if corrective action is needed. The goal of SPC is to prevent defects, reduce waste, and improve overall process efficiency.

SPC addresses the variations in the collected data, whether it is the production data, process data, equipment data etc.

All processes have some degree of variation. There are two types of variation: Common Cause Variation caused by natural, inherent variability in a process (random and predictable) and Special Cause Variation caused by unusual, unexpected variability caused by specific factors (e.g., machine malfunction, operator misoperation).

From the collected data, SPC calculates the control limits. Control limits represent the capability of a process, equipment, workstation, or procedure. It is calculated from the collected data from a given production unit, such as a workstation, to determine the range of variation statistically. Upper Control Limit (UCL) and Lower Control Limit (LCL) are typically set at ±3 standard deviations from the process mean.

Control limits are different from specification limits, which are used by design. If a data point is outside of specification, the process is wrong and the product may not work. Therefore, the control limits must be within the specification limits.

A process is said to be manufacturable, if it consistently produces output within specification limits. One important interface between the product design and factory is the "Design for Manufacturability". It is useless to do aggressive and stringent design that the machines in the factory are not capable of making. Therefore, the capability of the workstations and equipment in the factory must be passing to the design team in the form of control limits of each of the workstation and equipment.

SPC also shows the stability of a process. A process is considered stable (in control) if all data points fall within the control limits and show no non-random patterns.

Many tools are used in SPC to monitor the processes in the factory. These tools include Variable Control Charts for continuous data (e.g., dimensions, weight), Attribute

Control Charts for discrete data (e.g., defect counts, pass/fail), such as P-charts, C-charts, U-charts, Histograms, Pareto Charts, Scatter Diagrams.

SPC also generates indicators for process capability analysis, such as Cp, Cpk, Pp, and Ppk.

By using SPC, all the data in the factory become organized in such a way that it makes sense. It is like X-Ray in the health monitoring. By implementing SPC, organizations can achieve greater process control, improve product quality, and enhance customer satisfaction.

Section 4.12   Enterprise Resource Planning (ERP)

Enterprise Resource Planning (ERP) is a transformative tool that enables organizations to integrate and optimize their core business processes. By providing real-time data, automating workflows, and enhancing collaboration, ERP systems drive efficiency, improve decision-making, and support sustainable growth. It is a software system that integrates and manages core business processes across an organization. It provides a centralized platform for streamlining operations, improving efficiency, and enabling data-driven decision-making. Interfacing ERP with MES provides a bridge between production automation with the business automation system of a company.

ERP consolidates production data and business workflows into a single system, therefore, enables factory to share data with the businesses side of the company to streamline operations, improve efficiency, and make data-driven decisions. For example, the purchase requisition of the production raw materials initiated by the Warehouse Management System under MES passes to ERP for the workflow of the budget approval and starts the preparation of purchase order.

From finance and human resources to supply chain management and customer relationship management, ERP systems provide a unified platform for managing all aspects of a business.

ERP evolves from Material Requirements Planning (MRP) systems in the early 1990's. MRP was primarily used in manufacturing to manage inventory and production schedules. Over time, ERP evolved to encompass a broader range of business functions, including finance, HR, procurement, and sales.

Modern ERP systems are highly customizable and scalable, catering to businesses of all sizes and industries. With the advent of cloud computing, ERP solutions have become more accessible, affordable, and flexible, enabling organizations to deploy them with minimal infrastructure investment.

ERP systems integrate data and processes across various departments, eliminating silos and ensuring consistency. For example, sales data can automatically update inventory levels, and financial records can reflect real-time transactions.

ERP automates routine tasks such as payroll processing, order fulfillment, and reporting, reducing manual effort and minimizing errors. This allows employees to focus on higher-value activities.

ERP provides real-time visibility into business operations, enabling managers to monitor performance, track key metrics, and make informed decisions. Dashboards and analytics tools offer actionable insights for improving efficiency and profitability.

By streamlining workflows and eliminating redundant processes, ERP systems enhance operational efficiency and reduce costs.

ERP fosters collaboration by providing a centralized platform where employees can access and share information across departments.

With real-time data and advanced analytics, ERP empowers decision-makers to identify trends, anticipate challenges, and seize opportunities.

ERP systems improve customer service by enabling faster order processing, accurate inventory management, and personalized interactions.

Organizations that implement ERP gain a competitive edge by optimizing their operations, responding quickly to market changes, and delivering superior value to customers.

ERP systems automate and optimize functions such as finance, human resources, supply chain and manufacturing. Since manufacturing exists in the context of business, ERP serves as a bridge between factory and business.

For example, manufacturing cost data are sent to the financial system of the company, so as the product delivery, order of raw materials in the supply chain. It connects various departments and functions into a single unified system. It ensures real-time data sharing and consistency across the organization.

ERP systems are modular. Many modules are related to manufacturing, such as Supply Chain Management (SCM), Inventory Management, Procurement, etc. Once it is setup, all tasks are performed automatically. For example, if the inventory level of certain chemical in the factory warehouse is low, ERP will generate purchase order to the supplier automatically.

For a large manufacturing company with multiple factories, ERP system is usually Cloud-Based, which is hosted on remote servers, accessible via the internet (e.g., SaaS models like Oracle NetSuite, SAP S/4HANA Cloud). Smaller companies normally have On-Premise ERP installed locally on a company's servers and managed in-house. The cloud-based ERP system is getting more popular for its flexibility and scalability. Cloud-based ERP also allows to adopt AI and Machine Learning solutions.

By implementing an ERP system, organizations can achieve greater operational efficiency, improve decision-making, and gain a competitive edge in their industry. As businesses continue to navigate an increasingly complex and competitive landscape, ERP will remain a critical enabler of operational excellence and innovation.

Chapter V. Data Automation

Data automation refers to the use of technology to automate the processes of collecting, processing, analyzing, and managing data. It eliminates manual tasks, reduces errors, and accelerates data-driven decision-making.

Data automation encompasses:

- Data Collection: Automated tools gather data from multiple sources, such as APIs, sensors, and databases.
- Data Processing: Automated workflows clean, transform, and prepare data for analysis.
- Data Analysis: Algorithms and machine learning models analyze data to generate insights.
- Data Visualization: Automated tools create dashboards and reports to present insights in an understandable format.
- Data Management: Automated systems store, organize, and secure data for future use.

Data automation is essential for handling the scale and complexity of large quantity of data generated from a factory, enabling organizations to derive value from their data efficiently. Such large collection of data is sometimes known as Big Data.

Data automation and Big Data are deeply interconnected. Big Data provides the raw material, while data automation enables its efficient processing and analysis. Together, they create a powerful ecosystem for data-driven decision-making. For example:

- Real-Time Analytics: Data automation processes streaming Big Data in real-time, enabling businesses to respond quickly to changing conditions.

- Predictive Insights: Automated machine learning models analyze Big Data to predict trends, customer behavior, and operational risks.
- Scalability: Data automation ensures that organizations can handle the growing volume, velocity, and variety of Big Data without overwhelming their resources.

Section 5.01   Big Data

In today's data-driven world, organizations are generating and collecting vast amounts of data at an unprecedented scale. This explosion of data, often referred to as Big Data, has created both opportunities and challenges. To harness the full potential of Big Data, businesses are turning to data automation—a process that uses technology to collect, process, analyze, and manage data with minimal human intervention.

Data automation is part of the Big Data technology, which enables smarter decision-making, improving efficiency, and driving innovation.

Big Data refers to extremely large and complex datasets that cannot be effectively managed or analyzed using traditional data processing tools. It is characterized by the 3 Vs:

- Volume: The sheer amount of data generated by devices, sensors, social media, and business transactions.
- Velocity: The speed at which data is generated and must be processed.
- Variety: The diverse types of data, including structured (e.g., databases), unstructured (e.g., images, videos, logs), and semi-structured (e.g., JSON, XML).

In addition to the 3 Vs, two more dimensions are often considered:

- Veracity: The reliability and accuracy of the data.
- Value: The insights and business value derived from the data.

Big Data is generated and collected from many different sources, such as IoT devices, social media platforms, e-commerce transactions, and industrial sensors. When analyzed effectively, it provides actionable insights that can transform businesses.

Organizations will adopt robust data governance frameworks to ensure data quality, security, and compliance.

In the industry, data automation and Big Data are transforming industries by enabling smarter decision-making, improving efficiency, and driving innovation. From healthcare and retail to manufacturing and finance, these technologies are unlocking new opportunities and solving complex challenges.

As technology continues to evolve, the integration of data automation and Big Data will play an increasingly central role in shaping the future of businesses and society. By embracing these technologies, organizations can stay ahead of the curve and unlock the full potential of their data.

The manufacturing industry is in the midst of a digital revolution, and Big Data is at the forefront of this transformation. With the proliferation of sensors, IoT devices, and advanced analytics tools, manufacturers now have access to unprecedented amounts of data. When harnessed effectively, this data can drive operational efficiency, improve product quality, and unlock new opportunities for innovation.

Big Data in manufacturing refers to the collection, processing, and analysis of vast datasets generated across the production lifecycle. This section explores the role of Big Data in manufacturing, its key applications, benefits, challenges, and future trends, highlighting its potential to revolutionize the industry.

In manufacturing, Big Data encompasses data from production lines, supply chains, equipment sensors, customer feedback, and more. Advanced analytics tools, such as machine learning and artificial intelligence (AI), are used to extract actionable insights from this data.

Some major applications include Predictive maintenance, which we have discussed extensively. By analyzing data from sensors embedded in machinery, manufacturers can predict equipment failures before they occur.

Big Data enables manufacturers to improve product quality by analyzing data from production processes and identifying defects in real-time. For example:

Cameras and sensors capture data during production, and Big Data analytics detect anomalies or defects.

By correlating defect data with process variables, manufacturers can identify and address the root causes of quality issues.

Big Data enhances supply chain visibility and efficiency by integrating data from suppliers, manufacturers, and distributors. For example:

- Demand Forecasting: Big Data analytics predict customer demand, enabling manufacturers to optimize inventory levels and reduce waste.
- Real-Time Tracking: Sensors and IoT devices track the location and condition of goods in transit, ensuring timely delivery and reducing losses.
- Case Study: Procter & Gamble (P&G) uses Big Data to optimize its supply chain, reducing inventory costs by 10-15%.

In the Production Process Optimization, Big Data analytics can optimize manufacturing processes by identifying inefficiencies and recommending improvements.

Big Data also can play an important role in the product design and innovation, by enabling manufacturers to leverage customer feedback and market trends to drive product design and innovation. Analyzing customer reviews and usage data helps manufacturers identify areas for improvement and new product opportunities. Big Data analytics support generative design tools that create optimized product designs based on specified constraints.

Big Data will power digital twins, creating virtual replicas of physical systems for real-time monitoring and optimization.

Big Data will play a central role in the development of smart factories, enabling seamless connectivity and data sharing across the manufacturing ecosystem.

Big Data is transforming the manufacturing industry by enabling data-driven decision-making, improving efficiency, and driving innovation. From predictive maintenance and quality control to supply chain optimization and sustainability, Big Data is unlocking new levels of productivity and competitiveness.

As technology continues to evolve, Big Data will play an increasingly central role in shaping the future of manufacturing, driving the industry toward smarter, more sustainable, and more efficient operations. By embracing Big Data, manufacturers can stay ahead of the curve and unlock the full potential of Industry 4.0 and beyond.

Section 5.02   Data Automation and Manufacturing

Factory collects huge amount of data from the factory floor. All data are stored in the centralized server in the MES.

For companies with multiple manufacturing sites, data can also be stored in the Cloud or Edge.

Data automation refers to the use of technology to automate the collection, processing, and analysis of data without manual intervention. It eliminates repetitive, time-consuming tasks and ensures data accuracy and consistency.

In the last chapter, we have discussed how data are being analyzed and generate decisions for actions. The key to the right decision is the sound analysis. Data automation is the precursor to the development and deployment of artificial intelligence (AI). More and more, the analysis is done by AI-based algorithms.

Once the data is collected, data automation tools streamline the data for cleaning and preprocessing, ensuring that it is in a usable format for algorithms. Without efficient data automation, the process of preparing data would be time-consuming and error-prone.

Data automation in the factory uses many different algorithms to analyze and decipher the implication of these data, Automated systems can process and analyze data much faster than manual methods, making it feasible to work with big data.

Factory also requires real-time data processing, because many decisions need to be made in real-time. Data automation facilitates the continuous flow of data, enabling systems to make instant decisions based on the most current information available.

Data automation tools often come with capabilities to integrate data from various sources, ensuring that systems have access to a comprehensive dataset. Since the data are collected from many different sources, the first step in handling these data is to do the data integration, by combining data from disparate sources into a unified system.

Some data are not in the usable form, and the data processing step transforms raw data into usable formats. This interoperability is vital for creating models that can understand and analyze complex, multi-faceted problems.

ETL (Extract, Transform, Load) tools are essential for data integration processes, enabling organizations to extract data from various sources, transform it into a usable format, and load it into a target system such as a data warehouse or database. Some examples of popular ETL tools are Informatica, Talend, and Apache NiFi.

By leveraging the right ETL tool, organizations can streamline their data integration processes, improve data quality, and make data-driven decisions more effectively.

The data is further segregated into different categories for the use of different modules in the MES system.

For example, equipment data enables manufacturers to identify trends, patterns, and anomalies of particular equipment. By analyzing data such as machine performance, energy consumption, and maintenance history, manufacturers can gain insights into the health and efficiency of their equipment. This information can be used to optimize equipment settings, reduce energy consumption, and extend the lifespan of machinery. The predictive equipment maintenance program also relies equipment data to predict the equipment status and make decision whether the maintenance is required in real time.

The process data generated by the equipment, such as temperature, pressure, gas flow etc. falls into another category, These data are correlated to the quality data, product test data, defect rate data to determine whether the WIP receives correct process. These data will be used for tracing the defect/ mis-process root cause, and for the yield analysis.

Production data analysis involves the use of data automation tools to monitor and analyze the performance of the production process. By collecting data on factors such as production speed, defect rates, and downtime, manufacturers can identify inefficiencies and implement corrective actions. For example, if a particular workstation consistently experiences high defect rates, the system can flag it for further investigation and recommend process improvements.

Quality data analysis is essential for ensuring that products meet the required standards. Automated systems can collect data on product dimensions, weight, and other quality parameters during the production process. This data is analyzed in real time to detect deviations from the specified tolerances. If a defect is detected, the system can automatically reject the product or trigger an alert for manual inspection. This helps manufacturers maintain high levels of product quality and reduce the risk of recalls.

Product data analysis involves the use of data automation tools to analyze data related to the performance and usage of finished products. By collecting data from sensors embedded in products, manufacturers can gain insights into how products are used in the field. This information can be used to improve product design, identify potential issues, and develop new features. For example, in the automotive industry, data collected from vehicles can be used to identify common failure modes and improve the reliability of future models.

Different categories of data are fed into different algorithms for analysis and decision making. Machine learning, a subset of AI, relies heavily on data to train models. Data automation ensures that machine learning algorithms have a steady supply of high-quality data, which is essential for tasks like pattern recognition, predictive analytics, and natural language processing.

By automating repetitive and mundane data-related tasks, organizations can free up human resources to focus on more strategic activities, such as developing and refining AI models. This optimization leads to more efficient use of talent and accelerates the pace of AI innovation.

In summary, data automation lays the groundwork for AI by ensuring that data is collected, processed, and made available in a way that is conducive to the development of intelligent systems.

Section 5.03   Feedback and Feed Forward Process Control

Feedback and feed forward process control are two techniques used in the manufacturing line to manage and regulate processes using the data collected from the process. It is one of the many applications of data automation in the process control. Both approaches aim to achieve desired outcomes, but they differ in how they respond to disturbances and changes in the system. Here's a detailed explanation of each:

Feedback control is a reactive approach that adjusts the process based on the difference between the desired process value and the actual output. It continuously monitors the output and makes corrections to minimize the error.

Feedback control responds to errors after they have occurred. It uses a closed-loop system where the output is fed back and compared with the target process value.

The controller adjusts the process to reduce the error between the target and actual output. Feedback control can stabilize a system and reduce the impact of disturbances over time.

As an example, A thermostat measures the equipment operating temperature (output) and compares it to the desired temperature (setpoint). If there is a difference, the heating system in the equipment is adjusted to bring the temperature back to the setpoint.

On the other hand, feed forward control is a proactive approach that anticipates disturbances and adjusts the process before they affect the output. It uses knowledge of the system and potential disturbances to make preemptive corrections.

In such a feed forward loop, the controller adjusts the process based on predicted disturbances to maintain the desired output. Feed forward control can provide precise control if the system model and disturbances are well understood.

As an example, in the industrial heating process in a chemical plant, if a known increase in raw material flow rate is expected to cool the reaction, a feed forward controller can increase the heating in advance to counteract the cooling effect before it affects the reaction temperature.

In many practical applications, feedback and feed forward controls are used together to leverage the strengths of both approaches. This combined strategy can provide robust and precise control, especially in complex systems where disturbances are both predictable and unpredictable.

In a sophisticated reactor, feed forward control might adjust the heating based on predicted environment temperature changes, while feedback control fine-tunes the adjustments based on the actual reactor temperature readings.

By understanding and implementing both feedback and feed forward process control strategies, engineers can design more effective and efficient control systems tailored to the specific needs of their processes.

Section 5.04   Automatic Fault Detection

Automatic fault detection is a critical component in detecting faults on the factory floor. It enables the identification and diagnosis of faults or anomalies in real-time or near real-time. Its purpose is to prevent faults from causing real damage in the production line.

This process leverages advanced technologies such as machine learning, signal processing, data analytics, and artificial intelligence (AI) to monitor systems, detect deviations from normal behavior, and trigger alerts or corrective actions.

Automatic fault detection refers to the use of automated systems to identify abnormalities, malfunctions, or failures in equipment, processes, or systems. It aims to detect faults early to prevent system failures or downtime, reduce maintenance costs by enabling predictive or condition-based maintenance, improve system reliability and operational efficiency.

The automatic fault detection system relies on the monitoring of constant real-time operation data as compared to the baseline historical data, which represents the normal operating condition. Algorithms analyze the processed data to identify deviations from normal operation to determine the root cause of deviation.

The algorithm normally consists of many techniques to detect and define the deviation, such as Statistical Process Control (SPC), Rule-Based Systems, which uses predefined rules or thresholds to flag faults, or Machine Learning (ML), supervised or unsupervised learning, to classify or detect anomalies, if AI is available.

Once a fault is detected, the system may attempt to diagnose the root cause using many advanced techniques. These techniques range from traditional techniques to the modern AI powered techniques. Some of these techniques are:

- Model-Based methods use mathematical models of the system to predict expected behavior, and compare actual system behavior with model predictions to detect faults.
- Data-driven methods rely on historical and real-time data to detect anomalies.
- AI powered system using supervised learning: Trains models on labeled data, unsupervised learning and reinforcement learning.

Sometimes, a combine model-based and data-driven approaches are used.

On the factory floor, such techniques can detect faults in machinery, production lines, or robotic systems. Predictive maintenance is basically the most noted example. For example, it is used to identify bearing failures in motors using vibration analysis.

Once the fault is detected, the system generates alerts or notifications for operators. In the advanced systems, automatic corrective actions may be triggered (e.g., shutting down equipment, adjusting parameters).

Automatic Fault Detection allows early detection of the fault before they escalate into major failures.

The fault detection system is improving continuously with the advancement of technologies. IoT-enabled devices provide real-time data for more accurate fault detection. More and more, advanced AI models are being used to improve fault detection accuracy and adaptability. With the arriving of Edge Computing, it allows the real-time fault detection at the source of data generation. Virtual replicas of physical systems, as in the Digital twin, enhance fault detection and diagnosis.

In summary, automatic fault detection is a powerful tool for ensuring the reliability, safety, and efficiency of modern systems. By leveraging advanced technologies, it enables proactive maintenance and minimizes the impact of faults across various industries.

Section 5.05   Digital Twin in Manufacturing

One of the most important applications of AI in the manufacturing is the use of Digital Twin. A Digital Twin in manufacturing is a virtual representation of a physical asset, process, or system that mirrors its real-world counterpart in real time. It uses data from sensors, IoT devices, and other sources to simulate, monitor, and optimize manufacturing operations. Digital twins enable manufacturers to improve efficiency, reduce downtime, and enhance decision-making by providing actionable insights and predictive capabilities.

Digital Twin is composed of the real-world object (e.g., a machine, production line, or entire factory) being mirrored, and a virtual model, a digital replica of the physical asset.

Advanced algorithms analyze data to provide insights, predictions, and recommendations. But a Digital Twin can simulate these recommendations and quickly find out which recommendation works best. The system then implements the recommendation as decision. For example, if a factory wants to meet its product delivery obligation next month with the current factory loading situation, Digital Twin can quickly recommend a product mix that can meet the requirement and do better.

There are many applications of Digital Twin in the factory, such as Predictive Maintenance, Process Optimization, Product Design and Development, to test and validate product designs in a virtual environment before physical prototyping, Quality Control, to simulate supply chain operations to optimize inventory, logistics, and delivery.

By leveraging digital twins, manufacturers can achieve greater operational efficiency, reduce costs, and drive innovation, positioning themselves for success in the era of Industry 4.0.

Section 5.06   Design Automation

Not only manufacturing can be automated, so as product design. An automated product design system leverages advanced technologies such as artificial intelligence (AI), machine learning (ML), generative design, and computer-aided design (CAD) tools to streamline and optimize the product development process.

These systems enable businesses to create innovative, high-quality products faster and more efficiently by automating repetitive tasks, generating design alternatives, and optimizing for specific parameters like cost, materials, and performance.

Design automation seamlessly connects CAD/CAM software to create detailed, manufacturable designs. It automatically updates designs when input parameters change. When design is complete, Bill of Materials (BOM) is generated automatically and sent to the supply chain to source the raw materials. It recommends materials and manufacturing processes based on cost, sustainability, and performance requirements. It also reduces waste and ensures designs are economically viable.

AI algorithms can generate multiple design options based on input constraints (e.g., weight, strength, material). It explores innovative shapes and structures that may not be intuitive to human designers.

Automates testing of designs under various conditions (e.g., stress, heat, airflow) using virtual simulations. Identifies potential flaws and optimizes designs before physical prototyping.

The design of modern electronic systems, such as integrated circuit or printed circuit board, involves millions of components, intricate interconnections, and stringent performance requirements. CAD/CAM functionality is inadequate. Instead, Electronic Design Automation (EDA) is used due to the different nature of electronic system and integrated circuit.

These kinds of design require tasks like schematic capture, simulation, layout design, and verification, The system used to automate such design is called the Electronic Design Automation (EDA). EDA's are special design software used to design and analyze electronic systems, such as ICs, PCBs, and system-on-chip (SoC) designs. As electronic systems become more complex, the role of EDA tools has expanded to include advanced functionalities like power optimization, signal integrity analysis, and thermal management.

As the demand for faster, smaller, and more efficient electronic devices grows, the complexity of designing these systems has increased exponentially. EDA systems streamline workflows, reduce design cycles, and improve accuracy.

EDA simplifies the process of creating circuit schematics by providing libraries of components, auto-routing capabilities, and error-checking features.

EDA also verifies the functionality, timing, and power consumption of designs before fabrication by doing circuit simulation, and verification. In addition, automated placement and routing tools optimize the physical layout of ICs and PCBs.

Automated DFM tools built into EDA system interface with the factory system to ensure that designs can be manufactured reliably and cost-effectively.

AI and ML are increasingly being used to automate and enhance EDA processes. They can predicts design outcomes and identifies potential issues early in the design cycle. Uses AI to generate optimized design solutions based on specified constraints.

AI and ML will play an increasingly central role in automating and optimizing EDA processes, from placement and routing to verification and testing.

Cloud computing will enable scalable, on-demand access to EDA tools and resources, reducing the need for expensive on-premises infrastructure.

AI-powered generative design tools will create optimized solutions based on specified constraints, enabling faster and more innovative designs.

Automation supports the design of 3D ICs, which stack multiple layers of transistors to improve performance and reduce power consumption.

The automation of EDA systems enables faster, more accurate, and cost-effective design processes. From schematic capture and simulation to placement and routing, automation is streamlining workflows and driving innovation.

As AI, cloud computing, and other advanced technologies continue to evolve, the automation of EDA systems will play an increasingly central role in shaping the future of electronics design. By embracing automation, companies can stay competitive and unlock new possibilities in the rapidly evolving world of electronics.

CAD/CAM or EDA all operate in the same principle. They allow faster time-to-market, by reduces design iteration time and accelerates product development cycles, It minimizes material waste and optimizes production costs, encourages creative solutions by exploring a wide range of design possibilities, reduces human error and ensures designs meet precise specifications.

Design automation allows the collaboration among product designers, factory engineers, and supply chain managers happening in the central server or cloud. Automated approval process tracks design changes.

In conclusion, automated product design systems are transforming the way products are conceived, developed, and brought to market. By combining AI, generative design, and advanced analytics, these systems empower businesses to innovate faster, reduce costs, and stay competitive in a rapidly evolving market.

Chapter VI.Applications of Automation in Different Industries

Due to different nature of different industries, automation scheme is also different. For example, assembly line is different from chemical plant. Automobile factory is different from semiconductor fabs. In this Chapter, we will discuss some of the particularity of automation used in different industries. Their commonalities will not be discussed here.

Section 6.01　Automation in Chemical Industry

The chemical industry is one of the most complex and high-risk industry, requiring precision, efficiency, and stringent safety measures. Chemical industry handles large amount of gases and liquid chemicals, which are very often explosive, toxic, inflammable, corrosive and working temperature and pressure is high.

Automation has emerged as a game-changer in this industry, enabling manufacturers to streamline operations, enhance productivity, and ensure safety. By integrating advanced technologies such as robotics, artificial intelligence (AI), and the Internet of Things (IoT), automation is transforming how chemical plants operate.

Chemical plant is characterized by using highly sophisticated chemical process. Automation can help in the process control and optimization.

Automation systems, such as Distributed Control Systems (DCS) and Supervisory Control and Data Acquisition (SCADA), are widely used to monitor and control chemical processes. These systems ensure precise control of variables like temperature, pressure, and flow rates, optimizing production efficiency and product quality.

There are two types of production process in the chemical plant: batch process and continuous process.

Batch process is a method of production where materials are processed in discrete quantities or batches, rather than in a continuous stream. This approach is commonly used when producing smaller quantities of a product, when flexibility is required to switch between different products, or when the chemical reactions or processes require specific conditions that are easier to control in a batch-wise manner.

In a batch process, materials are processed in specific amounts (batches) that are processed together from start to finish. The process involves a series of steps (e.g., mixing, heating, reacting, cooling, and separating) that are performed in a specific sequence.

Batch processes are highly adaptable, allowing for the production of different products in the same equipment by changing the recipe or process parameters. The process is not continuous; it starts and stops with each batch. Each batch can be tested and verified for quality before proceeding to the next step or being released as a finished product.

The batch process proceeds in the following sequence: First, raw materials are loaded into the reactor or processing vessel. The materials undergo chemical reactions, mixing, heating, cooling, or other operations as required. During the process, process parameters (e.g., temperature, pressure, pH) are closely monitored and controlled. The finished product or intermediate is removed from the vessel. Finally, the equipment is cleaned and prepared for the next batch.

Production of pharmaceuticals (e.g., antibiotics, vaccines), specialty chemicals (e.g., dyes, adhesives), polymers, resins, coating and many others.

In contrast to batch processes, continuous processes involve uninterrupted production, where raw materials are continuously fed into the system, and products are continuously removed. Continuous processes are typically used for large-scale production of chemicals like petrochemicals, fertilizers, and fuels. In a petrochemical plant, continuous process is used in automated control of distillation columns, reactors, and cracking units. In refineries, continuous process is used to continuous monitoring and controlling of crude oil refining processes. In fertilizer production, it is used in the automation of ammonia synthesis and urea production.

In the food and beverage Industry, it is used for continuous pasteurization, mixing, and packaging processes. The pharmaceuticals industry uses automated control of continuous manufacturing processes for active pharmaceutical ingredients (APIs).

Automation in continuous processes in chemical plants is essential for ensuring efficiency, safety, consistency, and cost-effectiveness. Continuous processes involve the uninterrupted flow of materials through a system, where raw materials are continuously fed into the process, and products are continuously removed. Automation plays a critical role in monitoring, controlling, and optimizing these processes.

Automation in continuous process starts with installed sensors and instruments, such as thermocouples, pressure transmitters, flow meters, and analyzers, along the process line. They measure process variables such as temperature, pressure, flow rate, pH, level, and composition in real-time.

The data from sensors are monitored and analyzed to maintain process variables within desired ranges. Common used systems include Distributed Control Systems (DCS) for centralized control for large-scale processes, Programmable Logic Controllers (PLC) for discrete and smaller-scale control tasks.

The choice between batch and continuous processes depends on factors such as production volume, product variety, and process requirements. Automated batch processing systems ensure consistency, reduce human error, and improve repeatability. For example, programmable logic controllers (PLCs) automate the sequencing of steps in batch reactions.

Chemical industry is increasingly adapting AI-powered systems to enable advanced process optimization, predictive analytics, and autonomous decision-making. Virtual replicas of chemical plants in Digital Twin, allows for real-time monitoring, simulation, and optimization of processes. The use of Collaborative Robots (Cobots) working alongside humans, enhancing productivity and safety in chemical plants.

In conclusion, automation is revolutionizing the chemical industry by enhancing efficiency, safety, and product quality. While challenges such as high initial costs and cyber security risks exist, the benefits of automation far outweigh the obstacles. As technology continues to evolve, automation will play an increasingly central role in shaping the future of the chemical industry, driving innovation and competitiveness in a rapidly changing world.

Section 6.02 Automation in Automobile Industry

The automobile industry has long been at the forefront of technological innovation, and automation is one of its most transformative forces. From assembly lines to supply chain management, automation is revolutionizing how vehicles are designed, manufactured, and delivered. By integrating advanced technologies such as robotics, artificial intelligence (AI), and the Internet of Things (IoT), the automotive sector is achieving unprecedented levels of efficiency, precision, and quality. This section explores the role of automation in the automobile industry, its key applications, benefits, and future trends.

Automobile Industry uses robot extensively in the assembly line. Robots are widely used for tasks such as welding, painting, and assembly. Robotic arms equipped with precision tools perform repetitive tasks with high accuracy, reducing human error and increasing production speed.

Automation enhances quality control by using AI-powered vision systems and sensors to inspect vehicles for defects. Cameras and sensors identify surface imperfections, misalignments, or faulty components. Automated systems measure vehicle dimensions to ensure compliance with design specifications.

Automation enables predictive maintenance by using IoT sensors and AI algorithms to monitor equipment health. By analyzing data such as vibration, temperature, and pressure, manufacturers can predict equipment failures and schedule maintenance proactively, reducing downtime.

Automation streamlines supply chain operations by optimizing inventory management, demand forecasting, and logistics. Automated systems track raw materials and components in real-time, ensuring optimal stock levels. AI algorithms optimize delivery routes and schedules, reducing transportation costs and improving efficiency.

Section 6.03   Automation in Pharmaceutical Industry

The pharmaceutical industry is a critical sector that demands precision, compliance, and efficiency to ensure the safety and efficacy of drugs. Automation has become a cornerstone of modern pharmaceutical manufacturing, enabling companies to streamline processes, reduce errors, and meet stringent regulatory requirements. By integrating advanced technologies such as robotics, artificial intelligence (AI), and the Internet of Things (IoT), automation is transforming how drugs are developed, produced, and distributed. While most of the automation techniques used in the chemical industry applies to the pharmaceutical industry, there are some specific automation techniques for this industry, such as in the area of drug discovery and development:

Automation accelerates drug discovery by automating high-throughput screening and data analysis. Robotic systems can test thousands of compounds simultaneously, identifying potential drug candidates faster and more accurately. AI algorithms analyze vast datasets to predict drug efficacy and safety, reducing the time and cost of development. Laboratory is an important part of the pharmaceutical industry. Automation in the laboratories also improves efficiency. Laboratories use automated systems for tasks such as sample preparation, pupating, and data analysis. Automated liquid handlers and robotic arms improve accuracy and reduce human error in repetitive tasks.

In addition, automated systems are used in pharmaceutical manufacturing to ensure precision and consistency. For example: Automated machines produce tablets with precise dosages and uniform quality. Robots fill vials, syringes, and blister packs, ensuring accuracy and reducing contamination risks.

The requirements of regulatory compliance in the pharmaceutical industry are high. Automated systems ensure compliance with Good Manufacturing Practices (GMP) and other regulatory standards by maintaining accurate records, monitoring processes, and generating audit trails.

Automation is revolutionizing the pharmaceutical industry by enhancing efficiency, quality, and compliance.

Section 6.04 Automation in Food and Beverage Industry

The food and beverage industry is a highly competitive and fast-paced sector that demands efficiency, consistency, and adherence to strict safety and quality standards. Automation has become a critical enabler in meeting these demands, transforming how food and beverages are produced, packaged, and distributed.

By integrating advanced technologies such as robotics, artificial intelligence (AI), and the Internet of Things (IoT), automation is driving innovation and improving operational efficiency in the industry. This section explores the role of automation in the food and beverage sector, its key applications, benefits, and future trends.

Food and beverage industry uses many manufacturing processes as in the chemical industry. Therefore, the automation techniques in the chemical industry large apply to the food and beverage industry. There are also some unique automation techniques applied to the food and beverage industry, such as:

In the sorting and grading, automated systems sort raw materials (e.g., fruits, vegetables, grains) based on size, color, and quality using AI-powered vision systems.

Cooking and Mixing processes also use automated machines to control cooking temperatures, mixing speeds, and ingredient proportions to ensure consistent product quality.

Packaging is a critical area where automation ensures speed, accuracy, and compliance with safety standards. In addition, automated systems fill bottles, cans, and pouches with precise quantities of food or beverages and seal them to prevent contamination. Robots apply labels and print expiration dates or batch codes with high accuracy.

One important aspect of the food and beverage industry is the quality inspection for food safety. Automation enhances quality control by using sensors and AI-powered systems to inspect products for defects or contaminants. Automated metal detectors identify and remove contaminated products from the production line.

Furthermore, the stringent cleaning and sanitization requirement also demands automated cleaning systems, such as Clean-in-Place (CIP) systems, ensure that equipment is thoroughly cleaned and sanitized without disassembly, reducing downtime and improving hygiene. For example, CIP process must be part of the manufacturing process for the meat packaging plant in order to prevent potential bacteria contamination.

Clean-in-Place (CIP) is an automated method of cleaning the interior surfaces of pipes, vessels, process equipment, filters, and associated fittings without disassembling the equipment. It is widely used in industries where hygiene and sanitation are critical, such as food and beverage, pharmaceuticals, biotechnology, and dairy processing.

CIP systems are designed to clean equipment with minimal manual intervention, reducing labor costs and human error. Cleaning occurs without disassembling the equipment, ensuring that the system remains sealed and contamination risks are minimized. CIP systems use a combination of water, detergents, acids, alkalis, and sanitizers to remove soil, bacteria, and other contaminants. The process is consistent and repeatable, ensuring thorough cleaning every time.

CIP process is typically performed in several steps:

- Pre-Rinse: Removes loose soil and debris using water.
- Cleaning: Circulates cleaning agents (e.g., caustic soda, acids) to dissolve and remove residues.
- Intermediate Rinse: Flushes out the cleaning agents with water.
- Sanitization: Uses sanitizing agents (e.g., hot water, steam, or chemicals) to kill microorganisms.
- Final Rinse: Removes any remaining sanitizing agents with purified water.

CIP systems are fully automated and tailored to the specific needs of the equipment and the type of residue being cleaned, ensuring optimal performance and compliance with industry standards.

In the beverage industry, automated dispensing systems ensure precise mixing and serving of drinks, reducing waste and improving customer satisfaction.

Other industries using CIP process include pharmaceutical and biotechnology industries, cosmetics and personal care product manufacturing and chemical processing industries.

Section 6.05   Automation in Fashion Industry

The fashion industry, known for its creativity and rapid trends, is increasingly embracing automation to enhance efficiency, reduce costs, and meet the growing demands of consumers. From design and manufacturing to retail and supply chain management, automation is revolutionizing how fashion products are created, distributed, and sold. By integrating advanced technologies such as robotics, artificial intelligence (AI), and the Internet of Things (IoT), the fashion industry is becoming more agile, sustainable, and customer-centric. This section explores the role of automation in the fashion industry, its key applications, benefits, and future trends.

Automation is transforming the design process by enabling faster and more accurate prototyping. For example: 3D Design Software tools like CLO3D and Browzwear allow designers to create virtual garments, reducing the need for physical samples. AI-powered systems generate design options based on specified parameters, such as fabric type, style, and customer preferences.

Automation is streamlining garment production, improving efficiency, and reducing labor costs. Machines like SoftWear Automation's Sewbots can sew garments with precision, reducing the need for manual labor. Automated laser cutters precisely cut fabric patterns, minimizing waste and improving accuracy.

Automation enhances quality control by using AI-powered vision systems and sensors to inspect garments for defects. Cameras and AI algorithms identify flaws such as stitching errors, fabric defects, or color inconsistencies. Automated systems measure garment dimensions to ensure compliance with design specifications.

Automation optimizes supply chain operations by improving inventory management and logistics. Robots manage inventory in warehouses, ensuring efficient storage and retrieval of products. AI algorithms predict customer demand, enabling manufacturers to optimize production and reduce overstocking.

Automation is enhancing the retail experience by personalizing customer interactions and streamlining operations. AI-powered virtual fitting rooms allow customers to try on clothes virtually, improving online shopping experiences. Self-checkout kiosks and cashier-less stores reduce waiting times and improve convenience.

Automation supports sustainability initiatives by reducing waste and optimizing resource usage. Automated cutting systems optimize fabric usage, minimizing waste.

Section 6.06   Automation in Agriculture Industry

Automation in the agriculture industry, often referred to as smart farming or precision agriculture, involves the use of advanced technologies to optimize agricultural processes, increase efficiency, reduce labor costs, and improve crop yields. Automation is transforming traditional farming practices by integrating robotics, artificial intelligence (AI), Internet of Things (IoT), drones, and data analytics into agricultural operations.

Precision Farming is getting more popular these days. It uses GPS, sensors, and data analytics to monitor and manage field variability. In doing so, it enables precise application of water, fertilizers, and pesticides, reducing waste and environmental impact. Many tools, including soil sensors, weather stations, and yield monitors, are used to monitor the crops and their environment.

Self-driving tractors, harvesters, and planters that operate with minimal human intervention. Equipped with AI and computer vision to navigate fields and perform tasks like plowing, seeding, and harvesting.

Drones and UAVs (Unmanned Aerial Vehicles) are also used for crop monitoring, spraying pesticides, and mapping fields. These tools provide real-time aerial imagery to detect issues like pest infestations, nutrient deficiencies, or water stress.

Robots are used extensively for tasks like planting, weeding, pruning, and harvesting, instead of manual labors. Robotic fruit pickers and weed-removal robots that use AI to distinguish between crops and weeds are getting more popular.

IoT devices collect data on soil moisture, temperature, humidity, and crop health. This data is transmitted to farmers in real time, enabling informed decision-making.

Smart irrigation systems use sensors and weather data to optimize water usage. Smart irrigation can help to reduce water waste by delivering the right amount of water at the right time.

Wearable sensors and RFID tags track the health, location, and activity of livestock. Automated feeding systems ensure precise nutrition for animals.

Vertical Farming and Controlled Environment Agriculture (CEA) are another important development in the agriculture. Automated systems control lighting, temperature, humidity, and nutrient delivery in indoor farms. Robots handle planting, harvesting, and packaging in vertical farms. Vertical farming uses third dimension of space, therefore, can double or triple the output. In the controlled environment, crops are free from damaging weather patterns and insect to yield much better.

AI algorithms analyze data from sensors, drones, and satellites to predict crop yields, detect diseases, and recommend actions. Machine learning models help optimize planting schedules and resource allocation.

Automation is revolutionizing agriculture, making it more efficient, sustainable, and resilient to challenges like climate change and population growth. As technology continues to evolve, the adoption of automation in farming is expected to grow, helping to feed a growing global population.

Section 6.07   Automation in Entertainment Industry

Entertainment industry includes movies, gaming, content streaming, TV, music, performance and many others. Automation in the entertainment industry has significantly transformed how content is created, distributed, and consumed. From film production to live events and streaming platforms, automation technologies are enhancing efficiency, reducing costs, and improving the overall user experience.

There are many areas in the entertainment industry that automation and AI play an important role. First of all, AI tools like ChatGPT and DALL·E are being used to generate scripts, music, and visual art. Automation tools streamline rendering, motion capture, and special effects production.

AI-powered software automates tasks like scene detection, color correction, and even editing based on predefined styles.

In the film and TV production industry, automated camera systems can follow pre-programmed paths or track subjects in real time. Drones are extensively used for aerial shots and complex cinematography without the need for manual piloting. Background stages can all be generated using AR/VR without setting up expensive live stages. Deepfake technology creates realistic digital replicas of actors for films and ads.

Deepfakes are created using algorithms called Generative Adversarial Networks (GANs), which consist of two neural networks: a generator and a discriminator. These networks work together to produce content that is increasingly difficult to distinguish from real footage. It can create realistic computer generated image (CGI) characters in movies or video games.

Technologies like LED walls and real-time rendering (e.g., Unreal Engine) automate background creation and scene adjustments.

In the live events and performances, stage setting is automated to use robotic systems to control lighting, stage movements, and special effects during concerts, theater performances, and award shows. Automated systems create lifelike holograms of artists or entirely virtual performers (e.g., virtual influencers or AI-generated singers like Hatsune Miku). Automated ticketing systems and facial recognition for entry streamline event management.

Streaming and content delivery through the internet became a huge industry. AI algorithms analyze user behavior to recommend movies, shows, or music tailored to individual preferences. Automated tools detect and remove inappropriate or copyrighted content on platforms like YouTube and TikTok. Automation ensures videos are optimized for different devices and internet speeds.

In the gaming industry, algorithms create game levels, characters, and environments dynamically. Automated NPCs (non-player characters) with advanced AI provide realistic gameplay experiences. Automated bots test games for bugs and performance issues.

In the music production area, AI music composition tools like Amper Music and AIVA can generate music tracks based on user inputs. AI-powered software adjusts audio levels, removes noise, and enhances sound quality. Visual contents can use tools to generate 3D models and environments for VR/AR experiences. AI-driven narratives adapt based on user choices in immersive experiences.

During the live performance, automation tools control lighting, sound, and effects during concerts. Automating advertising and marketing can buy and place ads in real time based on audience data.

Using automation in the entertainment industry reduces labor and production costs, speeds up content creation and distribution, provides new tools for artists and creators, and improves User Experience.

Content streaming is a big business in the entertainment industry. Automation in the content streaming industry has transformed how media is produced, distributed, and consumed. By leveraging technologies like artificial intelligence (AI), machine learning (ML), and cloud computing, streaming platforms can optimize operations, enhance user experiences, and scale efficiently. Platforms like Netflix, Amazon Prime, and Spotify use AI to analyze user behavior and recommend content tailored to individual preferences. Automated systems create playlists or watchlists based on user preferences and trends.

Adaptive Bitrate Streaming (ABS) automatically adjusts video quality based on the user's internet speed to ensure smooth playback. Content caching uses AI to predict popular content and cache it on edge servers for faster delivery. Load balancing automatically distributes traffic across servers to prevent downtime during peak usage.

AI analyzes video and audio content to generate metadata (e.g., tags, descriptions, and thumbnails). AI also automatically categorizes content into genres, themes, or moods for easier discovery. Dynamic Ad Insertion (DAI) inserts targeted ads into live or on-demand streams in real time.

Content streaming companies are using varieties of automation to improve their services. For example, Netflix uses AI to recommend content, optimize streaming quality, and generate personalized thumbnails. Spotify creates personalized playlists like "Discover Weekly" using machine learning. YouTube automates content moderation using AI to detect and remove inappropriate videos.

Automation is reshaping the content streaming industry, enabling platforms to deliver richer, more personalized experiences while optimizing operations. As technology continues to evolve, the potential for innovation in this space is immense.Automation is reshaping the entertainment industry, enabling new forms of creativity and delivering more engaging experiences to audiences. As technology continues to evolve, its role in entertainment will only grow, offering exciting possibilities for the future.

Section 6.08   Automation in Business

Business automation refers to the use of technology to perform repetitive tasks, streamline processes, and improve efficiency within an organization. By automating manual or time-consuming tasks, businesses can reduce errors, save time, and allocate resources more effectively. Automation can be applied across various functions, including operations, marketing, sales, finance, and customer service.

The most obvious automation in the business is to automate the business process or workflow. These tools are known as the workflow management system. It is designed to help organizations automate, streamline, and optimize business processes. It ensures that tasks are completed in a structured, efficient, and consistent manner by defining, executing, and monitoring workflows.

The system allows users to create a visual representation of the workflow, including tasks, decision points, and dependencies. Tasks within the workflow are assigned to specific individuals, teams, or roles.

Notifications or alerts are sent to assignees when a task is ready for action.

The system automates the flow of tasks, ensuring that each step is completed in the correct order. It can trigger actions based on predefined rules or conditions.

For example, one of the most commonly used workflow is the purchase requisition. An employee submitting the purchase requisition needs to have justification, budget approval, and several layers of management approval. Eventually the requisition goes to the purchasing department, which identifies prequalified supplier and generates a purchase order.

There are many other examples, involving every aspects of action taken by the business, such as invoice approval, customer support, project management, leave requests.

Workflow systems often integrate with other tools (e.g., CRM, ERP, email, or document management systems) to streamline data flow and reduce manual input.

The system tracks the progress of workflows in real time, providing dashboards and reports for visibility.

Automated reminders and notifications keep participants informed about pending tasks, deadlines, or changes in the workflow.

A workflow is created by mapping out the sequence of tasks, decision points, and rules. For example, an approval process might include steps like submission, review, approval, and notification.

The workflow is initiated by inputting data (e.g., a new request, form submission, or trigger from another system). The system assigns tasks to the appropriate users or systems based on predefined rules. For example, in an employee onboarding workflow, HR might receive a task to prepare documents, while IT is tasked with setting up accounts.

Once a task is completed, the system automatically moves the workflow to the next step. Conditional logic ensures that the workflow adapts to different scenarios (e.g., "If the request is rejected, notify the requester").

Managers can monitor the status of workflows in real time, ensuring that tasks are completed on time and identifying any delays.

Once the workflow is completed, the system archives the process for future reference or auditing purposes.

By implementing a workflow management system, organizations can eliminate inefficiencies, improve collaboration, and ensure that business processes are executed smoothly and consistently.

Marketing automation is another application of the business automation. It automates repetitive marketing tasks like email campaigns, social media posting, and lead nurturing.

Likewise, workflows in sales, customer service, finance and accounting, HR and recruitment can all be automated.

Without question, workflow automation can improve business efficiency, reduce cost, improve accuracy, and bring many other benefits to the business.

By leveraging business automation, organizations can focus on strategic initiatives, improve productivity, and stay competitive in a rapidly evolving market.

Chapter VII. Future Trends in Manufacturing Automation

The future of manufacturing automation is shaped by emerging technologies such as artificial intelligence (AI), the Internet of Things (IoT), and advanced robotics. These technologies are expected to further enhance the capabilities of automated systems, enabling manufacturers to achieve even greater levels of efficiency, flexibility, and innovation.

AI-Powered Automation uses AI algorithms to analyze vast amounts of data to optimize production processes, predict equipment failures, and improve product quality.

The objectives of a factory is to improve productivity, to reduce cost, to improve quality, to minimize WIP, to improve the machine utilization and uptime, and many others.

Once the objective is defined, the factory sets to identify the operation that can impact the objective. For example, in order to improve the machine utilization, factory has to feed enough WIP and to reduce the downtime and overall maintenance time and to improve the throughput. Next, the factory has to identify what operation is needed to feed enough WIP to the equipment, and what actions need to be taken to reduce the equipment downtime, and to improve the throughput.

At this point, the factory needs to collect the data related to necessary operations and actions. By feeding these data into the algorithms, factory will be able to see the action and reaction – how certain actions improve the result and others degrade the results. The algorithms powered by AI will automatically optimize the actions, which are sent to the factory for execution.

By doing so for all the manufacturing objectives, the data automation will

Section 7.01   Lights-Out Factory

Lights-Out Factory is a fully automated manufacturing facility that operates without human presence on the production floor. The term "lights-out" refers to the idea that the factory can run in the dark, as no human workers are needed to oversee operations. These factories rely on advanced technologies such as robotics, artificial intelligence (AI), the Internet of Things (IoT), and automation to handle all aspects of production, from raw material input to finished product output.

All processes, including material handling, assembly, quality control, and packaging, are automated. Industrial robots are used extensively to perform tasks such as welding, painting, and assembly.

AI algorithms take over the responsibility of managing and optimizing production schedules, predict maintenance needs, and ensure quality control.

WIP's are transported by Automated Guided Vehicles (AGVs), or other types of transport systems.

There are many Lights-Out Factories in the world today. Some examples are: FANUC - A Japanese robotics company operates a lights-out factory where robots build other robots. Siemens - Has implemented lights-out production for circuit boards in its electronics plant. Tesla uses highly automated processes in its Gigafactories, though not fully lights-out. Philips operates a lights-out factory in the Netherlands for electric shavers.

By embracing lights-out manufacturing, companies can achieve unprecedented levels of efficiency, productivity, and innovation, positioning themselves as leaders in the era of Industry 4.0.

Section 7.02   AI in Manufacturing

Automation in manufacturing is transforming the industry by enabling manufacturers to achieve higher levels of efficiency, quality, and flexibility. Automation in equipment, factory and data plays a critical role in optimizing operations and driving innovation. While challenges such as high initial costs and workforce displacement remain, the benefits of automation far outweigh the drawbacks.

As emerging technologies continue to evolve, the future of manufacturing automation promises even greater advancements, paving the way for a new era of industrial excellence.

Integration of AI accelerators into manufacturing is already happening. AI enables smarter, more efficient, and adaptive production processes. AI is transforming how factories operate, reducing costs, improving productivity, and enhancing product quality.

AI is already entrenched in areas such as predictive maintenance, quality control and defect detection, process optimization, supply chain management, robotics and automation, generative design, human-machine interaction, inventory management and many others.

AI accelerators are increasingly being built into industrial hardware, enabling AI-driven operations like machine vision or process optimization. In the near future, edge AI, Digital Twins, and AI-driven customization, collaborative AI will also enter the mainstream applications.

AI is transforming manufacturing by enabling smarter, more efficient, and adaptive production systems. As the adaption of AI technology in the factory and business continues to increase, its impact will only grow, paving the way for the factories of the future.

Progress in the semiconductor chips provides ever more powerful computing power and more capable sensors to allow for better control and interface and to reduce latency in virtual PLC setups, highlighting a strategic alignment between hardware and software capabilities in industrial technology.

It is estimated that the overall industrial automation market — including hardware and software will be over $250 billion by 2024. At current rate of growth, the market may exceed $400 billion by 2027.

Section 7.03   Natural Language Processing and HMI

Human-Machine Interaction (HMI) can be greatly enhanced by the Natural Language Processing (NLP), since NLP makes the human to machine communication much easier.

NLP, a subfield of artificial intelligence (AI), focuses on enabling machines to understand, interpret, and generate human language. It has made tremendous progress in the recent years, driven by breakthroughs in machine learning architectures, data availability, and computational power.

These innovations have enabled machines to understand, generate, and interact with human language at unprecedented levels of sophistication.

The introduction of transformer architectures revolutionized NLP by leveraging self-attention mechanisms. These models process sequences of text in parallel and capture long-range dependencies in language. Architectures like GPT-4 and Google's BERT use Transformer Models to analyze entire conversational histories to grasp context, sarcasm, and implied meaning.

GPT-4 can generate coherent, context-aware text by analyzing entire input sequences. T5 (Text-to-Text Transfer

Transformer) treat all NLP tasks (translation, summarization, etc.) as text-to-text problems, simplifying training.

Transformers power chatbots (ChatGPT), search engines, and tools like GitHub Copilot, enable human-like interactions and code generation. Models adapt to new tasks with minimal examples, reducing reliance on extensive training data. Meta's NLLB and Google's Universal Speech Model support 1,000+ languages and dialects, democratizing access for non-English speakers.

Advances in NLP are poised to revolutionize Voice-based Human-Machine Interaction (HMI), enabling more intuitive, context-aware, and human-like communication between users and systems. By overcoming limitations in understanding intent, nuance, and multilingualism, modern NLP technologies are transforming voice interfaces into indispensable tools across industries.

Systems learn individual preferences and detect frustration or urgency in a user's tone to prioritize responses.

NLP is increasingly integrated with other data modalities (images, audio, video) to create richer AI systems. Systems like GPT-4V (Vision), Flamingo, and CLIP link text with visual data, enabling tasks such as image captioning, visual question answering, and content moderation. Advances in automatic speech recognition (ASR) and voice synthesis (e.g., OpenAI's Whisper, Google's WaveNet) have improved accessibility and real-time translation.

With the increasing power of Natural Language Processing (NLP), it has become a cornerstone of modern Human-Machine Interaction (HMI), enabling more intuitive, efficient, and human-like communication between users and machines. By bridging the gap between human language and machine understanding, NLP transforms how we interact with devices, systems, and software.

NLP allows machines to interpret and respond to natural language inputs (spoken or written), eliminating the need for rigid command-based interfaces.

Systems like Alexa, Google Assistant, and Siri use NLP to understand voice commands, answer questions, and control smart home devices.

NLP-powered chatbots engage in fluid conversations, resolving queries without human intervention.

Powered by NPL, workers can use voice commands to control machinery, improving safety and efficiency. NLP models analyze user preferences, historical interactions, and context to deliver tailored responses.

NLP offers many applications in the business automation. For example, streaming platforms (e.g., Netflix) and e-commerce sites use NLP to suggest content/products based on user language patterns.

In the business automation, NLP provides workflow automation: Employees can give instructs via tools like Zapier or Power Automate to do a workflow. For example: a manager can tell the system to call a meeting by specifying time, date, location, subject and list of attendants. A worker in the factory can tell the system to deliver certain parts to a specific workstation. This allows hands-free operation in workplaces.

Platforms like GitHub Copilot translate natural language prompts into functional code snippets.

The scope of interaction can be further expanded when combining NLP with vision, gestures, and AR/VR for immersive interactions (e.g., Meta's Project Aria).

NLP transforms HMI from transactional to conversational, making interactions with machines as natural as talking to another human.

By enabling voice-driven control, personalized assistance, and cross-language collaboration, NLP reduces friction, enhances productivity, and fosters inclusivity.

NLP is moving toward general-purpose language models that seamlessly integrate with robotics, IoT, and augmented reality (AR). Innovations in quantum machine learning and neuromorphic computing could further accelerate progress.

Ultimately, NLP aims to enable machines to understand not just language, but the intent, emotion, and context behind it—ushering in a new era of human-machine collaboration.

NLP and HMI are increasingly integrated to create more natural and efficient human-machine interactions. Advancements in AI, such as more sophisticated transformer models and multimodal interfaces, will further enhance NLP and HMI.

These technologies will continue to evolve, enabling more natural, efficient, and inclusive interactions between humans and machines, ultimately transforming how we live and work.

In the healthcare industry, voice assistants transcribe patient-doctor conversations, generate EHR notes, and remind patients to take medication. Amazon's AWS HealthScribe integrates NLP for clinical documentation.

Improved NLP is transforming voice HMI from a transactional tool into a context-aware, empathetic collaborator. By enabling machines to understand not just words but intent, emotion, and cultural nuance, voice interfaces will become seamless extensions of human communication. From healthcare to smart cities, the fusion of advanced NLP and voice HMI will redefine productivity, accessibility, and user trust—ushering in an era where talking to machines feels as natural as talking to a friend.

Section 7.04   Cloud Computing and Manufacturing

The manufacturing industry is undergoing a digital transformation, and cloud computing is at the heart of this revolution. Cloud Computing is playing an ever increasing role in the automation of manufacturing, driving the Future of Smart Factories.

By leveraging the power of cloud-based platforms, manufacturers can enhance operational efficiency, improve collaboration, and unlock new opportunities for innovation. Cloud computing enables the seamless integration of data, applications, and processes across the entire manufacturing ecosystem, from the factory floor to the supply chain.

Cloud computing refers to the delivery of computing services—such as storage, processing, analytics, and software—over the internet ("the cloud"). Instead of relying on local servers or physical infrastructure, businesses can access scalable, on-demand resources from cloud service providers like Amazon Web Services (AWS), Microsoft Azure, and Google Cloud. In manufacturing, cloud computing enables real-time data sharing, advanced analytics, and seamless collaboration across global operations.

Manufacturing generates vast amounts of data from sensors, machines, and production systems. Cloud computing provides a centralized platform for storing, managing, and analyzing this data. For example:

Cloud platforms can process large datasets to identify trends, optimize processes, and improve decision-making.

Manufacturers can store years of production data in the cloud for compliance, auditing, and analysis.

Cloud computing enables predictive maintenance by analyzing data from IoT sensors and equipment in real-time. The systems can monitor equipment health from anywhere, providing early warnings of potential failures. Cloud platforms can host AI models that predict equipment failures and recommend maintenance actions.

Cloud computing enhances supply chain visibility and efficiency by integrating data from suppliers, manufacturers, and distributors. For example:

Cloud-based systems can track the location and status of raw materials and finished goods in real-time.

AI algorithms hosted on the cloud can predict demand and optimize inventory levels.

Cloud computing facilitates collaboration among design and engineering teams, regardless of their location.

Engineers can use cloud-based computer-aided design (CAD) tools to create and share product designs. Cloud platforms enable virtual testing and simulation of product designs, reducing the need for physical prototypes.

In the production planning and scheduling, Cloud-based systems can optimize production planning and scheduling by analyzing real-time data from the factory floor. For example: AI algorithms can adjust production schedules based on changing demand, resource availability, and machine performance. Cloud platforms can optimize the allocation of materials, labor, and equipment to maximize efficiency.

In Quality Control and Defect Detection, Cloud computing enables real-time quality control by analyzing data from sensors and cameras on the production line. For example: Cloud-based AI models can analyze images of products to detect defects and ensure quality standards.

Cloud platforms can monitor production processes and identify deviations from target specifications.

Cloud computing supports remote work by providing access to critical applications and data from anywhere. For example: Cloud-based platforms like Microsoft Teams and Slack enable remote teams to communicate and collaborate effectively. Manufacturers can use cloud-based systems to monitor and control production processes remotely.

Cloud based manufacturing is still evolving, it can be expected that in the near future, several trends will emerge.

The combination of edge computing and cloud computing will enable real-time data processing at the source while leveraging the scalability of the cloud.

Cloud platforms will increasingly host AI and machine learning models, enabling advanced analytics and automation in manufacturing.

Cloud-based digital twins will create virtual replicas of physical systems, enabling real-time simulation, monitoring, and optimization.

We can expect that Cloud computing will play a central role in the development of smart factories, enabling seamless connectivity and data sharing across the entire manufacturing ecosystem.

Many companies have already used Cloud-based manufacturing extensively. For example:

Siemens uses cloud-based platforms like MindSphere to connect and analyze data from industrial equipment, enabling predictive maintenance and process optimization.

General Electric's Predix platform leverages cloud computing to provide industrial IoT solutions for asset performance management and operational efficiency.

Tesla also uses cloud computing to collect and analyze data from its vehicles and manufacturing processes, driving continuous improvement and innovation.

Procter & Gamble uses cloud-based analytics to optimize its supply chain and improve demand forecasting.

In conclusion, Cloud computing is transforming the manufacturing industry by enabling real-time data sharing, advanced analytics, and seamless collaboration. From predictive maintenance and supply chain optimization to collaborative design and energy management, cloud computing is unlocking new levels of efficiency, agility, and innovation. While challenges such as data security and integration complexities remain, the benefits of cloud computing far outweigh the obstacles. As technology continues to evolve, cloud computing will play an increasingly central role in shaping the future of smart factories, driving competitiveness and sustainability in the global manufacturing landscape. By embracing cloud computing, manufacturers can stay ahead of the curve and unlock the full potential of Industry 4.0 and beyond.

Section 7.05   Applying Edge AI in Manufacturing

The manufacturing industry is undergoing a profound transformation driven by advancements in artificial intelligence (AI), the Internet of Things (IoT), and edge computing. Among these technologies, Edge AI is emerging as a critical enabler of smarter, more efficient, and adaptive manufacturing processes. By deploying AI algorithms directly on local devices or edge servers, manufacturers can process data in real-time, reduce latency, and make faster, more informed decisions. This section explores the applications, benefits, challenges, and future trends of applying Edge AI to manufacturing, highlighting its potential to revolutionize the industry.

Edge AI refers to the deployment of AI models and algorithms on local devices, such as sensors, cameras, robots, and edge servers, rather than relying on centralized cloud infrastructure. This approach allows data to be processed and analyzed at the source of generation, enabling real-time insights and actions. In manufacturing, Edge AI bridges the gap between traditional automation and intelligent decision-making, empowering factories to operate with greater efficiency, flexibility, and precision.

Edge AI is used in many operations in manufacturing. In quality control, Edge AI is transforming how defects are detected and addressed. By embedding AI algorithms into cameras and sensors on the production line, manufacturers can inspect products in real-time with unparalleled accuracy.

Edge AI-powered vision systems can identify defects such as cracks, scratches, or misalignments in products as they move along the assembly line. AI algorithms can measure product dimensions and compare them to specifications, ensuring compliance with quality standards. Edge AI systems can learn from past inspections, improving their ability to detect new types of defects over time.

Robots are increasingly being used in manufacturing for tasks such as assembly, welding, and material handling. Edge AI enhances the capabilities of these robots by enabling them to make real-time decisions without relying on external servers. For example:

- Edge AI enables cobots to work safely alongside human workers, enhancing productivity and flexibility.
- Edge AI can optimize manufacturing processes by analyzing data from production lines and adjusting parameters in real-time. For example:
- Energy Efficiency: Edge AI systems can monitor energy consumption and adjust equipment settings to reduce waste.

- Yield Improvement: By analyzing production data, Edge AI can identify inefficiencies and recommend adjustments to improve yield.
- Dynamic Scheduling: AI algorithms can optimize production schedules based on real-time demand and resource availability.
- Edge AI can improve supply chain visibility and efficiency by tracking inventory and monitoring logistics in real-time. For example:
- Inventory Management: Edge AI systems can track raw materials and finished goods, ensuring optimal stock levels.
- Condition Monitoring: Sensors with Edge AI can monitor the condition of goods in transit, such as temperature-sensitive products, and alert stakeholders to any issues.
- Predictive Analytics: AI algorithms can predict supply chain disruptions and recommend mitigation strategies.

Edge AI is still evolving. The development of ultra-efficient AI models that can run on low-power microcontrollers will enable Edge AI to be deployed on even the smallest devices. Combining Edge AI with digital twins will create real-time virtual replicas of physical systems, enabling advanced simulation and optimization. Edge AI will enable mass customization by adapting production processes to individual customer requirements, driving innovation and customer satisfaction.

Edge AI is revolutionizing the manufacturing industry by enabling real-time decision-making, reducing latency, and enhancing efficiency. From quality control and predictive maintenance to autonomous robotics and supply chain optimization, Edge AI is unlocking new levels of productivity, quality, and sustainability.

While challenges such as hardware limitations and integration complexities remain, the benefits of Edge AI far outweigh the obstacles. As technology continues to evolve, Edge AI will play an increasingly central role in shaping the factories of the future, driving innovation and competitiveness in the global manufacturing landscape. By embracing Edge AI, manufacturers can stay ahead of the curve and unlock the full potential of Industry 4.0 and beyond.

Index